HAPPIER HUMAN

53 SCIENCE-BACKED HABITS
TO INCREASE YOUR HAPPINESS

S.J. SCOTT

ISBN-13: 978-1-946159-19-9

DISCLAIMER

YOUR FREE GIFT

As a way of saying thanks for your purchase, we're offering a free digital product that's <u>exclusive</u> to readers of *Happier Human*.

One of the best ways to get started is to build the "gratitude journaling" practice. So with that in mind, we are offering a free PDF version of our bestselling physical journal:

The 90-Day Gratitude Journal: A Mindful Practice for a Lifetime of Happiness.

To learn more, click (or tap) the image or link below to get free instant access.

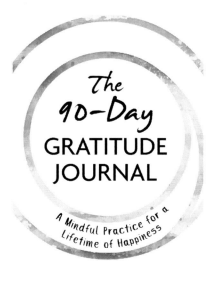

S.J. Scott & Barrie Davenport

>> Go Here To Get Your Copy of The 90-Day Gratitude Journal <<

www.developgoodhabits.com/90day-gratitude

Contents

PART 1:

YOUR HAPPINESS STARTS TODAY

Everyone wants to be happy.

If you ask a random person about what they want from life, they'll *usually* say something like, "I just want to be happy!"

Unfortunately, while happiness is a goal for most of us, it's also very elusive. People *say* they want to be happy, but their lives often seem at odds with this desired outcome.

Furthermore, happiness is next to impossible to quantify. It's not like you can create a goal like "I want to experience five units of happiness each day." Happiness is a nebulous emotion that can't be tracked or measured.

In fact, sometimes you're not even aware that you're experiencing one of the happiest moments of your life. It's only *years later* that you realize a specific event, memory, or experience was amazing. And then you might worry that you will never feel that level of positive emotion again.

On the other hand, while happiness is challenging to measure, there *are* a wide range of strategies that can help you increase your overall life satisfaction. In fact, you can boil them down to three simple rules:

1. Focus on the things that truly matter.
2. Eliminate (or minimize) what makes you unhappy.
3. Create habits that help you achieve both these outcomes.

Seems overly simplistic, right?

Well, as you'll see, there have been countless studies in the field of positive psychology (i.e., the study of happiness.) What they discovered is you *can* increase happiness—if you're willing to focus on the *right* habits.

Now, the question you might have is: *Why* should you concern yourself with happiness?

Well:

- A marriage with five times more positivity than negativity is significantly less likely to result in divorce.[1]
- A business team with five times more positivity than negativity is significantly more likely to make money.[2]
- College students with three times more positivity than negativity are significantly more likely to have flourishing mental health.[3]

In general, when a human system contains three to five times as much positivity as negativity, it is **significantly more likely to thrive**.

Simply put:

The results of over 200 scientific studies of nearly 275,000 people have found that happiness leads to success in nearly every domain of our lives, including marriage, but also health, friendship, community involvement, creativity, and our jobs, careers, and businesses.

Unfortunately, we now live in a world where it's increasingly difficult to be happy on a consistent basis.

In fact, our bodies were designed for an environment that has now disappeared. The ancestral conditions that designed our happiness switch have disappeared. At one time, the best

---

1   https://www.gottman.com/blog/the-magic-relationship-ratio-according -science/

2   http://www.factorhappiness.at/downloads/quellen/S8_Losada.pdf

3   https://www.ncbi.nlm.nih.gov/pmc/articles/PMC3126111/

thing you could do if you wanted happiness was to follow your emotions and instincts. That time no longer exists.

The modern world has broken our emotional guidance system. Emotionality that once helped us thrive now causes us to flounder and fail.

Let's consider two broken emotions: fear and anger.

At one point in time, the emotion of fear kept us alive. You saw a tiger, felt fear, and ran away; this helped you survive. Now let's imaging that you spent a few seconds thinking dispassionately instead of feeling fear. Odds are, you'd get gobbled up by Mr. Tiger.

Our conscious minds don't think fast enough. They evolved to help us build and execute long-term plans, not to escape deadly tigers running at 25 miles an hour.

Without fear, our ancestors wouldn't have been able to react fast enough—they would have died, and we would never have been born.

Nowadays fear is broken.

Because we fear rejection, we don't make the introductions and invitations that would create a rich social life. At one point, a person's tribe would have a few dozen people—100 or 200 maximum. A rejection meant a permanent loss. Now we have tens of thousands of potential friends, associates, and romantic partners to pick from. One rejection, even 100 rejections, means nothing. Yet we still experience frequent fear.

Now, consider anger.

Anger served to protect what was ours—our safety, our loved ones, our food, and our property.

Imagine you're living in a prehistoric, ancestral environment—tribes, tents, and spears.

You've caught your neighbor trying to steal your food supplies. Without the food, you'll starve during the upcoming winter.

You *could* let him off without punishment. After all, you caught him before he was able to eat your food. It's all still there, available to keep you alive.

In fact, without the emotion of anger, it's likely that you would let him off. You might tell him not to do it again, but you wouldn't punish him. **And then you'd die.**

Back then, it was a simple equation.

See Someone Stealing → Feel Anger → Punish Thief → Stealing Discouraged

If you let him off so easily, he's likely to try stealing your food again. The one time he succeeds, you and your family will die of starvation.

Can you imagine dispassionately assaulting the criminal, hurting him enough that he learns his lesson? I can't. That's what the anger was for.

Nowadays anger is more trouble than it's worth.

Because we have police and diplomacy and can have reasoned discussion, anger is rarely the best response.

If others aren't respecting our preferences, we ought to either compromise or get them to stop. But people don't respond well to anger. Usually, compassion and patience will get better results. Indeed, replace every instance of anger with compassion and patience, and our divorce rate would be cut in half.

Anger is a tool of brute force—a hammer where a screwdriver would work better. Some anger is good; it motivates us to take action. But if you're so angry that you're pushed to yelling? That's stupid. If at the end of the tears and pain there was change, the anger might be worth it. But the usual response is defensiveness and disinvestment.

My point here?

The cues and triggers that once kept us alive now keep us from reaching our potential—specifically when it comes to our overall happiness.

It's for that reason that **we have to take responsibility for our happiness** in ways we've never had to before, and it's for that reason that happiness offers such a large life advantage.

You can think of happiness like a gatekeeper. Those who have it are given access to a portion of their mental resources denied to everyone else. Creativity, compassion, and confidence—three emotions once widely experienced that led to great enjoyment and benefit—have now been locked away, available only rarely and in small amounts.

If evolution had kept up with modern times, we'd be experiencing significantly more positive emotion than we actually do.

We would feel more:

- Curiosity about people, cultures, languages, and the world around us

- Optimism to try new projects and explore different life paths
- Love for family, friends, and even total strangers

Unfortunately, the modern world has warped our minds. Despite our wealth and safety, we're:

- **Less healthy.** Yes, when cavemen got seriously sick, they died. Otherwise, they were tall and muscular.

- **Less social.** Yes, we have Facebook. But our ancestors spent most of their time with other humans.

- **More stressed.** Yes, we have food, shelter, and abundant water. But we've also got bills, taxes, demanding bosses, crazy children, and 1,000 other things to worry about.

- **Less satisfied.** Yes, we're tens of thousands of times richer. But success was once well defined. You either had food and friends, or you didn't. Now success has become a rat race. *There's always something more to be had.*

Each of us could benefit from more happiness and long-term investment, but because of this environmental mismatch, we're not getting it.

So, if you're someone who wants to break away from the confines of the modern world and increase your overall life satisfaction, I invite you to read the following book, *Happier Human: 53 Science-Backed Habits to Increase Your Happiness*.

About *Happier Human*

The premise of *Happier Human* is simple—you will discover 53 actionable habits to improve your happiness set point. Unlike many articles (or even books) you find online, these ideas aren't included just because they sound nice. This means you won't find shallow advice like: "Do what you love," "Hug a kitten," or "Take a long walk on a beach."

Instead, each idea is supported by a wealth of studies and research from the field of positive psychology. The only suggestions included are the ones *proven* to be useful. Odds are, if an idea helped someone else, it will help you as well.

Does this mean you need to adopt *all* 53 habits in order to feel happier?

Absolutely not!

It would be impossible to try every idea in this book and live a normal life. Instead, I suggest you think of this content like a buffet of options. Pick the ideas you like, learn how to implement them, and disregard everything else.

That said, I have identified what are called "the big levers of happiness." These are the strategies that countless studies have shown to be the biggest drivers of life satisfaction. If you dedicate yourself to *just* these nine habits, you'll notice a dramatic shift in your overall happiness. Fortunately, these will be the first batch of habits covered in this book.

Beyond the 53 habits, I will also cover: eight reasons many people experience unhappiness, specific strategies to implement each suggestion, and a simple process for creating a habit out of any happiness-related idea.

Focusing on happiness can help increase your career prospects, enrich your interpersonal relationships, improve your health, and provide more meaning for your daily grind. If these are outcomes you'd like to achieve, let me briefly introduce myself, and then we'll dive into the content.

About the Author

My name is Steve "S.J." Scott. I run the websites *Happier Human*[4] and *Develop Good Habits*[5] and have published dozens of books about personal development.

Like many people, I have struggled with happiness for much of my life. Most days are pretty good. But the bad days can be really, *really* bad. I'm talking about head-under-the-covers-never-leave-the-house kind of bad days.

For the most part, I've been able to "self-medicate" my happiness levels by understanding my different emotional triggers and building positive habits to manage the darker days when they occur. That's one of the major reasons I love writing about habits—because they personally help me regulate my moods.

One of these periods started in late 2015 and lasted most of 2016. After a string of weeks where I barely left the house and didn't accomplish anything beyond binge-watching Netflix, I realized I had to make a dramatic shift in how I approached life.

So, I did a few things:

First, at the suggestion of my friend and frequent coauthor, Barrie Davenport, I started to focus on mindfulness and meditation. I built a habit of spending more time in the present moment (instead of always being in my head). Heck, Barrie and I even

---

4 http://happierhuman.com/
5 https://www.developgoodhabits.com

wrote a few books on this subject, like *Declutter Your Mind*,[6] *10-Minute Mindfulness*,[7] and *The Mindfulness Journal*.[8]

Next, I completely overhauled many aspects of my life. I said no to any project (or request for my time) that didn't align with my values and goals. What's counterintuitive is I sometimes said no to projects that would generate a *lot* more money but would also add more stress and unhappiness to my life. Moreover, I also made the conscious decision to curtail my total working hours and spend more time with my son, who was born in April 2016.

Finally, as many people do, I researched what makes people happy. I read a number of books on the subject. I tried a variety of habits. And I conducted online research on different concepts on happiness.

It was during a random Google search that I came across a website called HappierHuman.com[9] run by a guy named Amit A (the coauthor of this book).

What struck me about this content was how much **time and effort Amit put into each article**. Instead of providing a series of strategies that *sounded nice*, he supported every idea with a wealth of science-based research. I fell in love with the content and used many of Amit's ideas in my personal life to slowly increase my levels of happiness.

I also noticed that he hadn't updated the website for over three years. I felt this was a shame because not only was his content

---

6   https://www.amazon.com/Declutter-Your-Mind-Eliminate-Mindfulness -ebook/dp/B01KU04K5A

7   https://www.amazon.com/10-Minute-Mindfulness-Habits-Living-Present -ebook/dp/B071HVMVVR

8   https://www.amazon.com/dp/1973531690

9   https://www.happierhuman.com/

excellent, it was also getting lost in the billion websites that populate the Internet. It was then I realized there was an opportunity to share this content in book form with a wider audience. So I emailed Amit, offering to buy his site.

Long story short, eight months and a bit of money later, I am now the proud owner of HappierHuman.com. To paraphrase the old Remington ad from the seventies, I liked the content so much, I bought the website.

So why should *you* care about this background information?

Simple: What you're about to read is a *blend* of the research-based strategies that Amit detailed on his blog and my experience in building habits. These are ideas that countless people (myself included) have personally used to increase their happiness set point. And not only will you discover a clear understanding of why a strategy is helpful, you will also get a quick action plan of how to incorporate it into your life.

Well, now that's out of the way, let's continue the conversation about happiness. Specifically, I'd like to dive into eight reasons why many people experience unhappiness—especially since most of us can easily meet our basic needs in life.

8 Reasons People Struggle with Unhappiness

In 1943, Abraham Maslow wrote a paper called "A Theory of Human Motivation" in *Psychological Review*.[10] One of the theories he proposed is a five-tier model, which best describes what motivates our behaviors and actions, commonly known as **"Maslow's Hierarchy of Needs."**

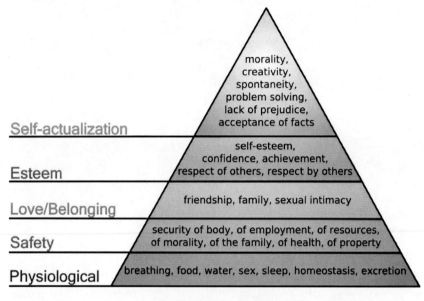

Image by *J. Finkelstein*[11]

The basic premise of this pyramid is you must satisfy basic needs before you can ascend to the next level. In other words, it would be ludicrous to worry about your meaning in life if you live in a war-torn environment where you struggle to meet basic needs

---

10   http://psychclassics.yorku.ca/Maslow/motivation.htm
11   https://commons.wikimedia.org/wiki/File:Maslow%27s_hierarchy_of
_needs.png

like food, water, and shelter. So that's why this hierarchy of needs is separated into two primary areas:

1. The bottom four levels are called *deficiency needs* (or *d-needs*) that motivate people. Once a d-need has been met, this desire will usually go away.

2. On the other hand, the top level represents *being needs* (or *b-needs*). These are about self-actualization. Even when these desires are met, there is still a desire to continue working on them.

In order of importance, these needs are as follows:

1. **Physiological needs,** which are the physical requirements for human survival. If these requirements are not met, the human body cannot function properly and will ultimately fail. This includes air, water, food, sex, clothing, and shelter.

2. **Safety needs,** which are protection from the elements, job security, financial security, and a safety net against catastrophic accidents or illnesses.

3. **Love and social belonging needs,** which relate to the feeling of interpersonal relationship. These include marriage, family, friendships, intimacy, and your immediate network.

4. **Esteem needs,** which relate to that desire to be respected by yourself and others. You typically gain this through a job, hobby, fame, or what value you provide to the world. You demonstrate esteem needs through mastery of a skill, achievement of goals, gaining status in a specific field, or earning respect from others.

5. **Self-actualization needs,** which are met at the top of the pyramid. This happens when a person reaches one's

full potential and frequently experiences peak moments throughout their lives.

What I find fascinating about Maslow's hierarchy is that it talks very little about money, consumerism, and the other trappings of modern society. Yet, these are the items that many people feel are important ingredients to happiness. In fact, if you carefully analyze Maslow's work, you will start to see some of the reasons many folks are unhappy nowadays. You can even boil them down into eight main reasons:

Reason 1: We constantly adapt to new "stuff."

We've all heard the expression that money can't buy happiness. But is that *actually* true?

The short answer: It depends!

In a Princeton University study[12] conducted in 2010 by psychologist Daniel Kahneman and economist Angus Deaton, the responses of 450,000 Americans polled by Gallup and Healthways in 2008 and 2009 were analyzed. The study determined that money *does* buy happiness—up to a specific point.

Financial security from money management reduces divorce rates, increases life span, and just plain feels good. Wealth purchases life-changing vacations, variety—the spice of life— and free time, with which to actually live life.

But the amount of money you *actually* need to be happy isn't as much as you probably think. The levels of happiness peak right

---

12   http://content.time.com/time/magazine/article/0,9171,2019628,00.html

around the $75,000 mark. (Eight years later, this number has increased to $105,000.)[13]

In other words, the average person in this study didn't report an increased degree of happiness. They've adapted. To them, a juicy steak tastes just a bit better than $1 ramen tastes to me.

So, the big lesson here is that money *can* buy happiness, but only when used in particular and often counterintuitive ways. (And when we get to the 53 strategies later on, I'll talk about how to strategically use money to "buy" happiness.)

That said, even though money isn't the answer, we are constantly bombarded by advertising messages that make us *believe* the secret to happiness can be found by purchasing a product. Daniel Kahneman[14] said it best:

> People are exposed to many messages that encourage them to believe that a change of weight, scent, hair color (or coverage), car, clothes, or many other aspects will produce a marked improvement in their happiness. Our research suggests a moral, and a warning: Nothing that you focus on will make as much difference as you think.

To illustrate this point, let's talk about the **power of adaptation**.

Imagine you're a college football star, on track to get drafted by a pro team. One day you get into an accident. You've been paralyzed from the waist down.

You'd be right in expecting that you'd feel terrible, like everything you'd been living for was now gone.

---

13   https://www.nature.com/articles/s41562-017-0277-0
14   https://www.amazon.com/dp/B00555X8OA

But slowly your desires and expectations would adjust. You'd stop dreaming of fame and football, and you'd start dreaming of other, more normal things, like getting married or buying a house. No doubt you'd have had a happier life if you hadn't become paralyzed. But don't underestimate your ability to adapt.

After a few years, many paraplegics feel almost as good as they did before becoming disabled. Many feel almost as good within a few months. Humans are remarkably adaptable. How else would we have taken over the whole world?

The problem with adaptation?

Now imagine you have what most people consider to be a "normal life." You've got a wife (or husband) and two kids. More than anything else, you want to get promoted. Because once you do, everything will change—you'll be able to replace your ten-year-old car, buy new clothes for your wife, and take your kids on vacation.

Being hardworking, you get that promotion. For a few days, maybe even a few weeks, you're living in wonderland. You're happy.

But then you notice your neighbor's car, a shiny $35,000 Lexus. You want it.

More than anything else, you want to get promoted. Because once you do, everything will change.

Being hardworking, you get that promotion. For a few days, maybe even a few weeks, you're living in wonderland.

But then ... and on, and on, and on.

Yes, as we get wealthier—and more famous, more powerful, and more beautiful—we get happier, but not nearly as happy as we'd expected.

All these experiences are best explained by a concept commonly known as the "hedonic treadmill" (or "hedonic adaptation").

The hedonic treadmill is a metaphor for your set point of happiness. The idea here is that when you purchase something that you *think* will make you feel happier, you will eventually return to your original emotional state. So if you're generally a happy person, a new possession won't make you significantly happier long-term. And if you're generally an *unhappy* person, purchasing the latest gadget won't lead to long-term happiness.

One study[15] often used to describe this phenomenon showed that despite their extreme joy in the moment, lottery winners were no happier than anyone else 18 months after winning the prize. People also return to this baseline feeling after getting married, buying a new house, and earning a job promotion, which are all things you would expect to permanently increase your happiness.

The term first appeared in Brickman and Campbell's essay "Hedonic Relativism and Planning the Good Society,"[16] published in 1971. The authors described people's tendency to remain at a baseline level of happiness regardless of any external events or changes in their demographic situations, such as getting married, increasing income level, or adding a new person to the family.

So while we've talked about how money can buy happiness in

---

15   https://web.archive.org/web/20160515201730/http:/members.ziggo.nl
/peterkooreman/pcl.pdf

16   http://www.oalib.com/references/7377976

certain circumstances, the hedonic treadmill explains why rich people aren't exactly happier than poor people, and why those who have very few material possessions and choose to live a simplistic life actually seem happier.

That's because the people who have only a few possessions are able to cherish what they have instead of taking them for granted. They are thankful for their belongings and are not constantly looking to find the "next best thing." The hedonic treadmill theory teaches us that long-term happiness is rarely influenced by major positive or negative events or life changes. You will go back to your happiness set point after you experience both good and bad things in life.

When it comes to material possessions, they eventually become something that you use habitually; therefore, you lose your appreciation for them. Once these items are no longer enjoyable, they deteriorate into needs instead of wants. This means that the amount of deprivation you feel without these once coveted items is greater than the amount of happiness you have possessing them.

For example, let's say a new smartphone is coming out in a few months and you just can't wait to have it. You figure that as soon as you get that smartphone, you will be such a happy person and all of your life's problems will subside.

The day comes when you get the phone, and you are excited to see how it's about to change your life. But after a few days, you're using this phone just as you were using your last one, and it hasn't seemed to impact your life at all. Instead of being this prize you've been waiting for, the phone is now just an everyday item you use.

On and on and on it goes as you keep buying more "stuff," hoping you'll eventually feel satisfied with that next purchase.

Reason 2: We struggle to meet our life expectations.

In American culture we respect and encourage wild dreaming: "You can become a millionaire! You can land a great job! You'll be promoted! You can write a best seller!" Children are encouraged to imagine being superheroes and fairy princesses. They play games in which, with little effort, they obtain power and save the world. They read novels where handsome, funny, and romantic men compete with each other to capture the affection of the protagonist, who is so normal that the reader can almost imagine being her. They watch tens of thousands of advertisements that promise them the world for just $10.

And then they encounter the real world: a 9-to-5 boring desk job, romantic partners with problems, and unchanging normality. All that dreaming comes at a cost.[17]

When the gap between expectations and reality grows too large, people become unhappy.

Their subconscious tries to fix the problem.

In an ideal world, their subconscious would say, "Your dreams are crazy, I'm going to adjust your expectations to where they should be."

In a less-than-ideal world, a person would start to overthink and temporarily feel even more unhappy. Feeling depressed, they

---

17   http://waitbutwhy.com/2013/09/why-generation-y-yuppies-are-unhappy.html

would give up on their crazy dreams. Now with more realistic expectations, they would bounce back and lead a happy life, free from overthinking. As crazy as this scenario seems, this is probably how things went hundreds of years ago—depression and overthinking were useful for fixing unrealistic expectations.

In the even less ideal real world, we try to have more realistic expectations and cultivate appreciation for what we already have, but modern culture and the hundreds of billions of dollars spent every year on advertisements refuse to leave us satisfied.

Advertising has done such a good job of controlling our thoughts that not only do we desire things we can't have, we feel entitled to them.

We feel entitled to have lots of money and a dream job, to have a consistently fulfilling relationship, to have our opinions listened to and respected by others, and to feel good most of the time.

When these expectations are violated, as they inevitably are, we do not easily accept it as a normal part of life; instead, we begin overthinking about why we are not getting what we deserve. Sometimes our ruminations focus on what is wrong with the world and why it's failing to provide us with what we want; sometimes our overthinking focuses on what is wrong with us that we can't accomplish our goals.

The entitlement obsession can lead to abundant overthinking: Why am I not progressing in my job? Why am I not rich? Why haven't I benefited from the economic boom of the last 10 years?

We answer these questions based on our sense of entitlement, by continuing to overthink even more:

Maybe it's because my boss is sabotaging my career for fear I will take his job.

Maybe it's because my parents wouldn't pay for me to attend an Ivy League college.

Maybe it's because my family responsibilities are holding me back.

Maybe it's because I'm not as smart as everyone else.

The truth is that reality is not as kind as your dreams. It's normal and okay to not get your promotion, to have a relationship that isn't working out, to feel bad every now and again.

If wishful thinking were harmless I'd encourage you to dream, dream, and dream some more.

But it isn't.

A large factor of happiness is expectations minus reality. Society encourages you to dream the world: you can be smarter, sexier, richer, and just plain better. What happens when you compare that dream against reality?

Reason 3: We fill our lives with chronic stressors.

Imagine your level of happiness like an iceberg. The tip of it is the immediate emotional, environmental, or conversational cue. You might think this is the main reason you're suddenly experiencing a negative emotion. But odds are, there is probably a wide range of hidden reasons you suddenly feel unhappy.

For instance, let's say you're feeling upset. You might *think* it's because you just had a fight with your significant other, but that's just one surface emotion that you're feeling. Perhaps your upset feelings are caused by a multitude of other issues lurking below the surface. Like:

- Poor sleep
- Lack of freedom at work
- Unrealistic expectations
- Hunched posture
- Recovering from a cold
- Financial insecurity
- Too much time spent sitting
- Overconsumption of sugar
- Mild sleep deprivation
- Rapid pace of life
- Vitamin deficiencies
- Lack of exercise
- Lack of sex

(To see a visual illustration of these points, check out this diagram from the Happier Human website.[18])

There are dozens of factors acting behind the scenes that influence your emotions. Skipping an hour of sleep once won't have much of an impact. But skipping an hour of sleep every weekday for weeks in a row? That's a low-level chronic stressor.

The lesson here?

The effect of low-level stressors is gradual. Since they don't

---

18   http://happierhuman.wpengine.netdna-cdn.com/wp-content/uploads /2014/05/Complexity-of-Emotion3.jpg

happen all at once, it's easy for people to not notice or even diminish their negative impact on levels of happiness.

Like the proverbial frog placed in cold water and then slowly boiled to death, it's easy to "get used to" mild annoyances until you wake up one day and they are suddenly a permanent part of your life.

These hidden stressors create and amplify negative emotions.

A rude comment from your romantic partner that usually would have been forgiven now triggers unhappiness, leading to unmanageable anger and sadness and causing a fight.

Worse, most chronic stressors are invisible to introspection.

No matter how long you spend thinking about the anger and sadness, your attention will keep coming back to the fight—to problems with your partner or perhaps to problems with you. The idea that the anger and sadness were caused by a poor diet or your three cups of coffee a day never comes to mind.

The main point here?

We often allow these chronic stressors to build up in our lives. You might not think they're a big deal, but over time, they add up to have a significant negative impact on your levels of happiness.

Reason 4: We have become addicted to technology.

The excessive use of gadgets, such as smartphones, tablets, and computers, has long been associated with numerous negative effects—specifically leading to depression and anxiety issues with many groups of people.

A recent study[19] by psychologists at San Diego State University revealed the link between prolonged screen time and the decrease in happiness levels among teenagers and adults.

Dr. Twenge's team revealed[20] that in 2012, when a large portion of the American population became owners of smartphones, people's happiness levels suddenly dropped. Teenagers were less satisfied with their lives, their friendships, the fun they derived from activities.

In the same study, adults also reported a decrease in general life satisfaction and frequency of sexual intercourse. Instead, the time they spent on their phones increased and continues to increase.

It also revealed that prolonged screen time propels young people to become unhappy—not unhappiness driving the teens to excessive screen time.

Furthermore, another study[21] led by Dr. Twenge uncovers the link between the increase in suicidal tendencies and depression and the excessive use of gadgets.

The reasons people become unhappy are varied. Considering that the bulk of screen time is usually spent on social media,[22]

19   http://psycnet.apa.org/doiLanding?doi=10.1037%2Femo0000403
20   https://patch.com/us/across-america/why-screen-time-making-you-unhappy
21   https://www.sciencedaily.com/releases/2017/11/171114091313.htm
22   https://www.twinword.com/blog/how-people-spend-their-time-on-the-internet-infographic/

however, this could be the culprit for increasing levels of unhappiness for the following reasons:

- **People compare themselves with others when they browse social media news feeds.** One person[23] commenting on Dr. Twenge's book described the use of social media as "validation hunting." Psychologists have identified the tendency to compare ourselves with others prevents us from being happy.

- **Social media becomes a substitute for face-to-face interactions.** Spending excessive amounts of time on social media robs us of the opportunity to create meaningful and actual connections with other people.

- **People have become sleep deprived.** The biggest time-sink when using social media is during the hour (or hours) before bedtime. Sleep is essential for health and well-being. So when you deprive yourself of sleep, you're actually setting yourself up for unhappiness.

Is there a solution? The study done by Dr. Twenge reveals that completely abstaining from screen time is not the optimal solution. Just limiting the screen time to no more than a couple of hours per day is enough to start restoring people's happiness levels. (We'll talk more about how to do this in the section that covers bad habits that cause unhappiness.)

Reason 5: We believe "quick fixes" work for happiness.

Self-help articles promise that you can fix your troubles in five easy steps.

---

23   https://www.amazon.com/gp/customer-reviews/R2H2V81ARL6AXL/

They're lying. Unfortunately, they have little choice.

"Success will take you 40 hours spread out over 25 steps. Also, there's a 50% chance of failure."

Who would read that?

People purchase *The Secret* expecting life transformation.

With a book like this, they go from thinking, *I have to work hard to have money*, to *Money comes easily and frequently*.

If only. That's not how the world works. But wanting a quick fix, people are willing to believe.

When the money doesn't come rolling in, they start overthinking, *Is there something wrong with me? Am I not trying hard enough? Are my thoughts too negative? Does God not like me? Should I wait longer?*

The problem isn't that they expect quick fixes. Quick fixes actually work most of the time. For instance:

- Need to eat? Buy food from your supermarket.
- Need to travel to your supermarket without walking three miles? Drive a car.
- Need to talk to someone hundreds of miles away without writing a letter and waiting weeks for a reply? Use your phone.

We have systems in place that mass produce quick fixes. **The problem is that we've overgeneralized the lesson. Yes, quick fixes work—but only *most* of the time, not *all* the time.**

When a problem remains unsolved after a few days, we assume something must be wrong, and we start overthinking.

If we're down or blue or upset, there must be some quick fix. Change our job, change our relationships, stop talking to our parents. Sometimes these are the right choices, but if they are done as a quick fix for dissatisfaction, they tend to accumulate into a string of failures that gives us more to overthink about, which leads us to the next challenge.

Reason 6: We often ruminate and overthink everything in life.

More and more people are getting fat. It's obvious when you consider the growing waistlines and increasing rates of cardio-vascular disease. We call it the *obesity epidemic*.

But there's another growing epidemic that's just as bad.

Why is the rate of depression on the rise?

Why do we feel more stressed than ever before?

There's a rumination epidemic.

In fact, 20% of Baby Boomers, 52% of Gen Xers, and 73% of Gen Yers ruminate excessively.[24]

What is rumination?

Rumination happens when you repeatedly think about a negative comment about your work performance. Or you frequently replay scenes of a job interview that went badly. Or you incessantly replay the climax of an argument with your teenage daughter, where she blurted out that you're a bad parent.

If you have a tendency to do such things, you are ruminating.

---

24   http://happierhuman.wpengine.netdna-cdn.com/wp-content/uploads /2014/05/Explaining-the-Gender-Difference-in-Depressive-Symptoms.pdf

Scientists categorize rumination as a negative type of reaction,[25] considering that those who engage in it dwell on negative emotions, their causes, and the numerous unpleasant results rather than proactively solving the problem.

Rumination is obsessing about negative remarks about you or your actions, your past mistakes, or other negative events that happened in the past. In psychology, rumination could be a sign[26] of the onset or presence of mental health illness.

Rumination takes form when you:

- Go over a failure or conflict again and again to see how it could have gone better
- Rant and rave about the wrongs that have been done to you
- Try to figure out why life isn't living up to your expectations
- Constantly reflect on your sadness
- Feel like your lifestyle is limited because of all the mental junk that's built up

Rumination can be very limiting because it directly impacts your emotions in a negative way. It creates negative thought loops. It leaves you feeling isolated. Even worse, when you're focusing on rumination, you're likely to push people away. All of these consequences of rumination can wreak havoc on your levels of happiness.

---

25   https://www.ncbi.nlm.nih.gov/pmc/articles/PMC4414423/
26   https://www.wsj.com/articles/worrying-about-the-future-ruminating-on
-the-pasthow-thoughts-affect-mental-health-1439223597

Reason 7: We often delay our gratification for the future.

All of your life you've been schooled in the philosophy of delayed gratification.

- Birth to College: Study even though you hate to. You need to get a good job!
- First Working Years: Get your boss his damn coffee! You need a promotion to pay off your debt and buy that house to impress your friends and family.
- Mid-life: Work, work, work, work! Mid-life crisis? Finding meaning in your work? I don't think so, honey. We need to save for the kids.
- Competitive 50s: Nest egg is too small! Work more!
- Retirement: Have fun, push your boundaries, develop strong social connections, and become genuinely happy?
- Afterward: Die.

I don't know about you, but this sounds like a hamster-wheel approach to life. Instead of living in the present moment, you're constantly focusing on the next step in the process in order to reduce fear and increase security.

That said, according to the Warwick University Worker Productivity study[27] and the Wesleyan Income study,[28] happier people are 10% to 20% more productive and earn on average $10,000–$30,000 more than their less jubilant peers.

So, which option sounds better to *you*?

27   http://www2.warwick.ac.uk/fac/soc/economics/research/centres/eri/bulletin/2009-10-3/ops/
28   http://www.iwu.edu/economics/PPE19/1Como.pdf

Ambition → Greater Productivity → More Money → More Happiness?

Or

More Happiness → Greater Productivity → More Money?

In the income study, the participants were asked questions to rate their happiness in 1979, when they were 14 to 22 years old. This single data point explained thousands of dollars in income disparity over the next 31 years of their life. *Don't mix up the order—it's happiness first.*

Reason 8: We think it's selfish to focus on happiness.

"If you're sad, deal with it or go see a shrink. If you're 'normal,' go on living your life as you already have been."

Unfortunately, this is the attitude of most Americans.

As an example, Gretchen Rubin of The Happiness Project[29] experienced resistance like this from all corners of her life when she decided to focus on her personal happiness.

Her husband didn't understand the need, and her friends thought she was being selfish. She constantly heard some version of the question: "Isn't having a good husband and two kids enough?"

It's easy for people to misconstrue your attempt to increase your happiness. When you have a job, family, bills, and other "adult" responsibilities, it's easy to feel like focusing on positivity is self-indulgent—perhaps even downright *selfish*.

Happiness comes from many sources: pleasure, certainly, but also from living with meaning, acting according to your values,

---

29   http://www.happiness-project.com/

volunteering, achieving your goals, showing gratitude, having strong social connections, and being engaged with your community.

In fact, as you'll discover in the 53 habits section, many of the keys to happiness come from helping others and positively affecting the world around you. And if you'd like to learn more about how happiness is *not selfish*, I encourage you to read the following:

- 29 Ways to Show Unique Gratitude[30] – Showing gratitude is the opposite of selfishness.

- Kindfully + Mindfully[31] – It's not "Treat others as you want to be treated," but "How you treat others is how you treat yourself." When you're kind to others, it's not just the recipients that have a better day.

- Stoicism 101[32] – Acting with virtue is not about repressive discipline but about being 100% proud of yourself.

- Happiness is contagious in social networks[33] – Happiness spreads to people three degrees removed from each other. A happier world starts with you.

- Voluntarily Happy[34] – Helping others is one of the most effective ways to grow and cultivate happiness. It's also a good way to develop your social network.

30   http://liveyourlegend.net/29-ways-to-show-unique-gratitude-and-other -random-acts-of-kindness/

31   https://zenhabits.net/kindfully/

32   http://hackthesystem.com/blog/stoicism-101-a-quick-guide-to-the -philosophy/

33   http://www.cnn.com/2008/HEALTH/12/05/happiness.social.network /index.html

34   http://www.goodhousekeeping.com/health/wellness/health-benefits-of -volunteering

Do these actions sound "selfish" to you?

Not to me.

2 Tools to Test Your Happiness

So far, we've talked in general terms about happiness. By now, you understand why it's important to work on this aspect of your personal growth and how it impacts multiple areas of your life in a positive way.

But what I *haven't* done is help you answer a very simple question:

"How happy are you right now?"

This might *seem* like a straightforward question. However, answering it can be challenging because we humans are constantly bombarded by an avalanche of emotions, experiences, stressors, tasks, and interactions with the world around us. So, one moment you might feel happy as can be and then 10 minutes later you'll feel down.

My point here?

While I feel it's impossible to determine your current level of happiness with 100% accuracy, there are a few tools you can use to get a good "guesstimate" of how you're currently feeling.

So in this section, we'll talk about one tool you can use to assess your happiness (the Losada Ratio) and a quick formula (mentioned in the book *The Happiness Hypothesis*[35]) that helps you understand how some people always seem to be happy.

---

35   https://www.amazon.com/dp/B003E749TE/ref=dp-kindle-redirect ?_encoding=UTF8&btkr=1

Tool 1: The Losada Ratio (aka: "The Positivity Ratio")

The Losada ratio (also known as the positivity ratio, Gottman ratio, and Losada line) is the sum of the positivity in a system divided by the sum of its negativity.

The positivity ratio came from the field of marital stability and relationship analysis, specifically from the research of John Gottman.[36] Over the course of dozens of studies and thousands of observations, he gained the ability to predict with over 90% accuracy whether or not a couple would divorce. A key factor of that prediction was the ratio of positive expressions to negative expressions.

The positivity ratio was then studied in the field of organizational psychology, from the research of Marcial Losada.[37] Adopting Gottman's coding methodology for business teams, Losada observed teams of eight while they developed strategic plans.

Once again, the ratio of positive expressions to negative expressions was highly predictive of team success, as judged by both hard numbers, like profitability, and soft numbers, like evaluations by colleagues and superiors.

The study that finally brought the positivity ratio to its current level of popularity came from the field of positive psychology, from the research of Barbara Fredrickson.[38] She found that college students with a positivity ratio above 3 were significantly more likely to have high mental and social health.

---

36   https://www.gottman.com
37   http://losada.socialpsychology.org/
38   https://fredrickson.socialpsychology.org/

These findings have been subsequently confirmed in additional settings (e.g., a nursing home), having been cited over 700 times. (That said, in the interest of full disclosure, this ratio has also been debunked in a follow-up study.[39])

What's my ratio, and what does it mean?

Whether or not you buy into the idea that happiness can be measured, you might want to spend a few minutes to test your positivity ratio, in order to better understand what makes people happy.

To get started, you can use this website to take the test:

https://www.positivityratio.com/single.php

In general, Losada and others have discovered that a 3.0 to 6.0 score has been found to be highly correlated with high performance. The higher your ratio the better.

Now you might wonder:

Can I increase my ratio?

Absolutely!

As you'll see, there are dozens of positive psychology strategies and habits you can use to increase your positivity ratio.

As an example, when I first took this test, I was at a 2.1. But then I spent over six months implementing a few strategies that we'll cover next—mostly from the "big levers" section. And now, as I'm writing this section, I just tested at a 3.2. Not a *huge* improvement, but definitely in an upward direction.

---

39   https://www.the-scientist.com/the-nutshell/positivity-ratio-debunked
-38894

Tool 2: The Haidt Formula

In the book *The Happiness Hypothesis: Finding Modern Truth in Ancient Wisdom*,[40] Jonathan Haidt talks about a simple formula you can use to determine your overall happiness.

Happiness (H) = Biological set point (S) + Conditions of your life (C) + Voluntary Activities (V)

Or

$H = S + C + V$

While you can't "self-test" this formula like the Losada ratio, I feel it can be used to get a basic understanding of how to improve *your* personal levels of happiness.

So, let's go over each of the three elements:

Biological Set Point (S)

The biological set point, unfortunately for those that weren't born with bundles of joy and enthusiasm (like myself), is an extremely strong beginning.

One study found:[41]

> Twin studies generally show that from 50 percent to 80 percent of all the variance among people in their average levels of happiness can be explained by differences in their genes rather than in their life experiences.

That's right, 50–80% of our life happiness is explained by genetic factors, essentially outside our control. (Fortunately, the reason

---

40   https://www.amazon.com/Happiness-Hypothesis-Finding-Modern
-Ancient-ebook/dp/B06XCF7WFR

41   https://www.ncbi.nlm.nih.gov/pmc/articles/PMC2593100/

this book exists is because science has also validated that there are proven ways to permanently increase our happiness.)

Conditions of your life (C)

Increasing happiness doesn't occur by getting that new car or big house you've been dreaming of. Because the hedonic treadmill has shown that we quickly adapt to new things, new toys, furniture, electric devices, homes, and refrigerators. You might experience increased joy for a few days, weeks, or months, but then you'll go back to your biological set point.

But Haidt found that three life conditions will have a dramatic positive or negative impact on your levels of happiness. In his words:

1. **Commuting:** "Many people choose to move farther away from their jobs in search of a larger house. But although people quickly adapt to having more space, they don't fully adapt to the longer commute, particularly if it involves driving in heavy traffic. Even after years of commuting, those whose commutes are traffic-filled still arrive at work with higher levels of stress hormones."

2. **Lack of control:** "Changing an institution's environment to increase the sense of control among its workers, students, patients, or other users was one of the most effective possible ways to increase their sense of engagement, energy, and happiness."

3. **Relationships:** "The condition that is usually said to trump all others in importance is the strength and number of a person's relationships. Good relationships make people happy, and happy people enjoy more and better relationships than unhappy people. Conflicts in relationships—having

an annoying office mate or room-mate, or having chronic conflict with your spouse—is one of the surest ways to reduce your happiness. You never adapt to interpersonal conflict; it damages every day, even days when you don't see the other person but ruminate about the conflict nonetheless."

Voluntary Activities (V)

The variable shows there are three classes of voluntary activities to consistently increase levels of happiness:

1. **Expressing gratitude** and kindness is a way to fight adaptation effects. If we start taking something good for granted, it stops giving us joy. If we express gratitude, we can reverse that process.

   In Haidt's words: "Studies that have assigned people to perform a random act of kindness every week, or to count their blessings regularly for several weeks, find small but sustained increases in happiness. So take the initiative! Choose your own gratifying activities, do them regularly (but not to the point of tedium), and raise your overall level of happiness."

2. **Meditating** and employing mindfulness techniques to enjoy the present, rather than ruminating on the past or stressing about the future, can boost mood both in the short term and long term.

3. **Engaging in flow** and pursuing our strengths has been associated with increased levels of satisfaction. Specifically, flow is a matter of arranging your day and your environment to increase both pleasures and activities that truly engage your mind.

So, there you have it—two tools to measure *your* current level of happiness. Hopefully, they helped you understand a bit more about life satisfaction and what you can do immediately to get more from each day.

Well, now that you know a little more about the research into happiness, let's dive into the 53 habits you can incorporate into your day. We will start first with a brief overview of how I've categorized these strategies then we'll dive into the heart of this book.

How *Happier Human* is Structured

The rest of this book is straightforward—53 habits broken down into four main sections.

The "Big Levers" of Happiness

Let's be honest here; some strategies will work better than others. So instead of forcing you to guess about what areas to focus on first, I've dedicated the first section to the habits that will have the biggest impact on your personal growth and happiness. These are called the *big levers* because even if you implement *just* these ideas, they will have a significant positive impact on overall life satisfaction.

The interesting thing? In countless studies, time and time again, these are the strategies that have been found to help people enjoy life a little more. So if you'd like a "quick win" from this book, I'd suggest focusing exclusively on these nine ideas.

Finding Happiness with Others

One of the simplest ways to create happiness is to build a strong support network of friends and family—this is even true for introverts. Once again, in countless studies, it was found that one of the major keys to happiness is to share experiences with the important people in your life and engage in vibrant conversations. With that in mind, I've dedicated a section to how you build a strong support network in your life.

Finding Happiness by Yourself

On the other hand, there are a variety of habits you can incorporate into your life in order to feel a little happier every day. Some of them are simple actions that only require a couple minutes of time each day, while others might require a completely new way of thinking about your life.

Finding Happiness by Eliminating Bad Habits

We all have our fair share of bad habits, but sometimes these routines can have a serious negative impact on our overall quality of life. In other words, sometimes the key to happiness isn't to *add* something to your life but to *subtract* something from it. With this section, I will profile over two dozen bad habits you should consider minimizing or eliminating.

One last thing: You'll discover there are a *lot* of links in this book. Most are to various books, websites, and research articles that support the claims I make about each idea. If you're unsure about the science, or you simply want to know more, I recommend you check out this additional information.

Well, that's a brief overview of the 53 habits we'll cover in this book. I urge you to review each one first, focus on the ideas that personally resonate with, and use the last section to build these happiness habits into your life.

Let's get started.

PART 2:

THE "BIG LEVERS" OF HAPPINESS

1. Use the 80/20 Rule to Focus on Happiness

One of the simplest ways to become happier is to focus on the actions that give you maximum results with minimal effort.

Put simply: If you apply the 80/20 rule to your entire life, you can strip away the things that create unhappiness and focus on what truly matters.

What is the 80/20 Rule?

This is a concept that was originally mentioned by Italian economist Vilfredo Pareto (this is why it is often referred to as the Pareto Principle). Pareto wrote that in economics, 80% of your results often come from 20% of your efforts. What's amazing about this discovery is that it has proven to be true in almost every real-world situation where it has been applied.

The 80/20 rule can be applied to any industry or business. For example, in general, 80% of revenue is generated by 20% of the salespeople; 80% of complaints come from only 20% of customers; and 80% of highway traffic is funneled through 20% of the roads.

It can also be applied to all the areas of your life.

Right now, only a handful of the activities you do each day or week have the biggest impact on your life—whether you're at work, at home, or enjoying a hobby.

The key lesson of the Pareto Principle is to be constantly intentional with how and where you spend your time.

No matter what tasks and obligations you need to do each week, there will always be a handful that leave you feeling happy and aligned with your purpose.

The trick is to identify these activities and focus on them instead of worrying about the activities that leave you feeling drained. The great thing about this principle is that, once you're mindful of it, you learn to focus on the 20% that yields the best results.

How can you apply the 80/20 rule to your life?

The answer is simple: create a habit where you examine each area of your life by asking 80/20 questions.

You can do this during a weekly review, when you feel over-whelmed, or when you feel like you change things up in your life.

80/20 for Your Career

You probably spend *at least* a third of your life at work—not even including the time it takes you to get there. So a quick "win" to increase your happiness is to focus on a strategy or two that will help you find more value at your current job.

Here are a few questions to ask yourself:

- What tasks do I enjoy doing every day? How can I spend more time working in this area?
- What tasks do I hate working on? How can I eliminate (or delegate) them?
- What core habits have had the biggest positive impact on my career?
- Are there tasks that my boss feels are most important to the success of my job?

- What items are causing the most distraction from focusing on my vital few?
- How can I add a little more enjoyment to my working day?

80/20 for Your Personal Finances

Personal finance is often the biggest stressor in life, and it's also one of the biggest causes of divorce. So, if you apply the 80/20 rule to your finances, you will probably decrease some of the unhappiness in your life. With an 80/20 focus here, you look for ways to: save for retirement, improve your credit score, eliminate your credit card debt, and invest in building long-term wealth.

Here are a few questions to ask yourself:

- What are the debts with the highest percentage interest?
- How can I eliminate those high-interest debts first?
- What actions on my part will generate the most revenue?
- How can I do more of my high-revenue-generating tasks?
- What are the top "leaks" when it comes to my spending?
- How can I cut my biggest expenses in half (e.g., getting a roommate to offset the cost of monthly rent/mortgage, carpooling to reduce gas expenditures, etc.)?
- What can I do to daily improve my credit score (since this is the one metric that directly impacts the interest rates that you end up paying)?
- What is the simplest investing strategy that will have the best long-term impact (e.g., investing in low-fee index funds through Vanguard)?

80/20 for Your Health and Fitness

Being "dialed in" to your health and fitness is yet another way to prevent unhappiness in your life. And this becomes especially important whenever you're experiencing chronic pain or a major illness.

So applying the 80/20 rule here is about maintaining a balance of physical fitness and eating the right foods. There are many sub-categories that are included here, like losing weight, improving your diet, eating different types of foods, and becoming more physically active.

Here are a few questions to ask yourself:

- What good habits can I create that will have a lasting positive impact on my health (like drinking water, tracking my food portion sizes,[42] or getting a good night's sleep)?

- What distractions, barriers, or habit triggers can I eliminate that prevent me from focusing on the healthy habits that I know I need to prioritize?

- What are my worst bad habits that I can eliminate, which have the biggest negative impact on my life (e.g., smoking, drinking, eating junk food, etc.)?

- What is the simplest exercise program that I know I can stick with at least three to four times per week?

- What are my biggest food weaknesses?

- What can I do to reduce unhealthy food from my life (e.g., creating a barrier to eating it by not keeping it in your home)?

- What events or activities cause my biggest weaknesses

---

42 https://www.developgoodhabits.com/portion-control-containers/

when it comes to eating (like holiday gatherings, work parties, or late-night drinking sessions)?

- What can I do to reduce or eliminate my tendencies to break down during these events?

80/20 for Your Leisure and Fun

Participating in fun activities like planning vacations, spending time with your family, or focusing on a hobby like home brewing, hunting, cooking, or painting is one of the true keys to happiness.

I will admit that sometimes leisure activities may not be the best thing to track, measure, analyze, poke, and prod. Sometimes leisure is just for ... leisure.

But you might want to consider looking at your life to make sure you're spending recreational time on the things that actually matter.

Here are a few questions to ask yourself:

- What activities do I enjoy most in the world?
- How can I get more benefits from these hobbies?
- How can I eliminate the physical possessions that don't have meaning in my life?
- How can I purposefully plan more enjoyable activities into my week?
- How can I get more of fun while on vacation, and less of the vacation "hassle"?
- If 80% of my truly energizing sleep comes from 20% of my time sleeping, how can I get more of that key rest time?
- What television programs (or other forms of media) can I

eliminate that I really don't enjoy? What online and offline subscriptions can I eliminate that I don't use?

- What are the 20% of my possessions that I use 80% of the time?

As a society, we tend to default to buying the latest, greatest things when it comes to recreation and leisure. But if you think about it, most of our fondest memories usually involve a special trip or time spent with the important people in our lives. So if you take time to do an 80/20 analysis, you might discover a better way to spend your limited free time.

80/20 for Your Relationships

Yes, relationships are a major source of happiness. And yes, you can use the 80/20 rule to enhance your relationship with your significant other, family members, or friends. In fact, you could also set goals to improve your social skills, find a romantic partner, or simply become a better person to everyone you meet.

Here are a few questions to ask yourself:

- Who are the people that cause 80% of my enjoyment and make me feel truly engaged?
- How can I spend more time with these people?
- Who are the five people I spend the most time with?
- Does the time I spend with these people make me better or worse?
- Who are the people I spend 20% of my time around who cause me 80% of my unhappiness, anger, and anxiety?
- How can I reduce time spent with them, or even completely remove them from my life?

- How can I spend more time with the 20% of people in my life who I get 80% of my enjoyment from being around?

- How can I connect with more people who share my interests?

- How can I do more of these things?

- How can I reduce or eliminate the actions that truly anger my significant other?

One last question:

Who are the people I spend 20% of my time with that cause 80% of my unhappiness, anger, and anxiety?

In one of my favorite quotes of all time, Jim Rohn said, "You're the average of the five people you spend the most time with."

This means if you take the time to do an 80/20 analysis, you can make sure that you're building relationships with the right people while also strengthening relationships with your loved ones.

80/20 for Your Service and Volunteering

Using the 80/20 rule for service is about having a bit of efficiency when you help others. It includes volunteering, supporting your favorite charity, or donating money to causes you believe in.

Here are a few questions to ask yourself:

- What are the few causes I truly support?

- What system can I create to support them (through volunteering or making donations) on a monthly basis?

- Who are the 80% of people who don't volunteer in my

church or house of worship, and how can I get them involved?

- How can I guide other people in my life to help out?
- What is the simplest way I can influence others who don't get involved?
- How can I set up an automated system for donating money to my favorite cause?

80/20 Rules for Your Spirituality

Finally, the 80/20 rule can be applied to the catch-all category of "spirituality." In the broadest terms, you can apply this principle in a variety of areas like mindfulness, meditation, prayer, yoga, or basically any activity where you're living in the present moment.

Here are a few questions to ask yourself:

- What bad habits are causing me the most unhappiness (e.g., scrolling through Facebook and getting worked up by a headline)?
- What tasks are causing 80% of my problems and unhappiness?
- What experiences produce 80% of my fulfillment and happiness?
- What do I do daily that makes me happy? How can I do more of it?
- What causes the most stress in my life? How can I do less of it?
- What small daily habits can I add to increase my level of happiness (e.g., meditation, getting outdoors, calling a friend, etc.)?

Keep the 80/20 rule in mind when you want to improve different aspects of your life. What you'll discover is that it's not hard to drill down to the essence of an activity to identify a few key habits you can do regularly. And once you focus on these activities, you'll find it's not hard to focus on what truly matters.

2. Subtract Unhappiness from Your Life

One of the simplest ways to apply the 80/20 rule to happiness is to eliminate much of what causes unhappiness in your life.

Obviously, you can't get rid of *all* your stressors because sometimes you have to go to a job you don't like very much or do monotonous household chores or deal with an unpleasant personal situation. Overall, though, you dramatically increase your life satisfaction by radically reducing the amount of "stuff" in your life—in order to free up the mental bandwidth for the people and experiences you truly value.

This isn't just pithy advice that sounds good on paper. Many successful people have given similar advice.

Warren Buffet famously said,[43] "The difference between successful people and really successful people is that really successful people say no to almost everything."

On a personal note, I applied this strategy in recent years, and it dramatically improved my happiness. Instead of accepting every offer that came my way, I said no to a bunch of things like public speaking gigs, side projects that were a distraction, people who didn't add value to my life, and every business opportunity that didn't perfectly align with my current goals.

The truth is there's only so much time in a day. In fact, it's impossible to keep cramming new stuff into your life without reaching a breaking point where you're stressed out and unhappy.

---

43 https://medium.com/the-mission/how-to-say-no-and-achieve-billionaire -success-with-warren-buffets-2-step-rule-4054b9437774

Eliminating what's not important will free up your mind and time to allow you to focus on what is important.

Here are a few strategies you can use to build the habit of saying no to the unimportant things in your life.

Identify What to Subtract

Take a hard look at your day-to-day routine to identify what might be causing unhappiness (or prevent you from focusing on what's truly important). We're all different, so we each have our own distinct set of vices. That said, I recommend you consider these activities, which might be causing unhappiness:

- Watching *hours* of TV every day
- Doing the chores you don't enjoy (i.e., *if* you have the funds, hire someone to handle chores like cleaning your house or landscaping)
- Agreeing to activities that you secretly hate but somehow feel obligated to do
- Getting rid of possessions you don't need
- Surrounding yourself with digital noise, including social media, news sites, apps, and other forms of addictive technology
- Playing videos games nonstop
- Drinking with your friends until late at night
- Maintaining low-value relationships that create negativity in your life
- Focusing on emotions (like anger, envy, or jealousy) toward people who don't have a direct impact on your life

- Engaging in negative self-talk that causes limiting beliefs and prevents you from going after what you truly desire

To get started, create a journaling habit for a week. The goal here is to track time spent on your various activities and how you feel about each one. When you see a common theme where the same person or experience creates negativity in your life, that's probably what needs to be immediately eliminated (or at least minimized).

Also, if you're having trouble tracking certain behaviors associated with technology, you can use tools like Rescue Time,[44] Moment[45] for iPhone, and Quality Time[46] for Android to help you monitor your use of technology. Each provides a simple report on how much time you're *actually* spending in front of a screen.

Ask Important Questions

Sometimes it's really hard to know, with 100% certainty, if a person or experience adds value to your life. That's why I recommend asking yourself important questions *every day*, like:

- Do I feel drained or energized when talking to a specific person?

- Do I feel drained or energized when engaging in a specific activity?

- Does this activity or person add value to my life, or does he/she/it cause conflict with my important goals?

- What would happen if I completely eliminated this activity from my life (or stopped talking to this person)?

---

44   https://www.rescuetime.com/
45   https://inthemoment.io/
46   http://www.qualitytimeapp.com/

- How can I delete or minimize an activity *without* ruining certain relationships in my life?

This is the time to be honest with yourself. If you feel like a person or experience conflicts with what's important, now is the time to take aggressive action to eliminate or minimize it.

Replace a Negative with a Positive

It's easy to default to a negative routine whenever you feel bored or disinterested. So if you identify a bad habit that's creating negativity, a surefire way to eliminate it is to focus on building a positive habit instead.

For instance, here are a handful of strategies to replace the experiences I mentioned before, which often cause unhappiness:

- Replace one hour of television each day by focusing on an activity related to an important goal.

- Build a practice where you identify the activities you don't enjoy and decide to delegate or delete them from your life.

- Set aside 10–15 minutes a day to go room-by-room and get rid of the possessions you don't need.

- Minimize the digital noise in your life by leaving all technology at home (i.e., your phone) and spending a daily hour outside.

- Identify the people who matter most in your life and plan regular experiences with them.

I'll admit that following the advice in this section requires *massive effort* on your part. But when you focus on what's truly important (and delete everything else), you'll discover a significant increase in happiness when compared to others who ignore the obvious things that are emotionally draining.

3. Live with Purpose

In the book *The Happiness Advantage*,[47] Shawn Achor discovered the following in his research:

> We've been taught that if we work hard, we will be successful, and then we'll be happy. If we can just find that great job, get a raise, lose those five pounds, happiness will follow. But recent discoveries in the field of positive psychology have shown that this formula is actually backward: happiness fuels success, not the other way around.

Furthermore, Achor makes the following point:

> When we are positive, our brains become more engaged, creative, motivated, energetic, resilient, and productive. This discovery has been repeatedly supported by research in psychology and neuroscience, management studies, and the bottom lines of organizations around the world.

In other words, having a sense of purpose provides meaning to your life. And if you focus on cultivating a happy life (before everything else), odds are you'll create greater success in multiple areas of your life.

Now, like you, I live in the real world, where I have bills to pay, a family to support, and numerous "adulting" responsibilities. So while I could tell you to find your dream job, I don't think this advice would be very practical. Instead, I feel you have two basic

---

47   https://www.amazon.com/Happiness-Advantage-Positive-Brain-Success -ebook/dp/B003F3PMYI/

choices: 1. Look for a job that gives you purpose and meaning. 2. Find meaning outside of your job.

Let's talk in more detail about each of these options.

Option 1: Find a Job That Gives You Purpose

How do you find the best job that matches your purpose? Here are a number of strategies you can use:

- **Write down** your personal mission statement.[48] This will ultimately serve as a guideline for all of your habits, routines, decisions, and future goals.

- **Review or identify your purpose.** What do you intend to do or contribute? Once you've found your purpose,[49] you can search for jobs that are aligned with your personal mission.

- **What is your personal definition of fulfillment?** This term is different for everybody. Does it mean living a certain lifestyle? Helping others improve their quality of life? Being famous for something? Writing down your thoughts can help steer you to the right direction to take in your career.

- **What skills do you possess?** List all the skills you've learned or acquired through experience or education.

- **What work experiences (jobs) have you had so far, and what were your main responsibilities in each?** You can list them in chronological order; you can also indicate if you were promoted to a position. Doing this helps you uncover more skills and abilities that you've overlooked the first time.

---

48   https://www.developgoodhabits.com/personal-mission-statement/
49   https://greatergood.berkeley.edu/article/item/how_to_find_your_purpose_in_life

- **List the things that spark your interest.** Do you enjoy helping people realize their potential, or are you more comfortable working alone and pondering the mysteries of the universe or writing code? If you're stuck figuring out what excites you, taking a personality test can assist you in discovering what makes you feel pumped up and excited.

- **Make a "jobs wish list."** List the key elements of your ideal job (e.g., the type of people you'd want to work with, the type of service or product quality that matters to you, the work environment and style of the company or organization, and the results you want to see). Go for the jobs that meet at least 70%, and higher, of your criteria.

- **Focus on the big picture when looking for a job that reflects/matches your purpose.** For example, if you want to be an entrepreneur to help provide jobs to others, you must be prepared to do activities that seem to be outside the scope of your dream career, such as preparing financial reports, engaging in sales and marketing, and dealing with human resources, to name a few. Do not be afraid of grunt work, especially if it's part of what it takes to get and keep your dream job.

- **Take a personality/career-matching test.**

  - If you are stumped in identifying your purpose (or if you have a broad range of interests), taking a personality-profile and career-matching test can help you pinpoint the jobs that fit your personality.

  - These are available online for free or for a minimal fee, and the results are usually available in less than an hour. Well-known tests include the most-used

Meyers–Briggs Type Indicator,[50] the MAPP Career Test,[51] and the Riso–Hudson Enneagram Type Indicator.[52]

Next, I recommend using the top websites to look for jobs related to your personal interests and passions. Here is a list of the top websites that can help you find that dream job.

- **GameChangers 500**[53] **[GC500]** – According to Forbes,[54] this website features "the world's top purpose-driven organizations using business as force for good." This site contains a list of companies (link to company profile, name, location, mission), their purpose, practices, link to the company's jobs page, and contact details.

- **80,000 Hours**[55] – the website of an organization dedicated to helping young people match their potential with the best jobs that have a positive impact on society at large. The site also has an excellent resource for career advice. More importantly, it has a curated job board[56] that lists available jobs addressing "the world's most pressing problems" (according to their website).

- **Headhunter.com**[57] – experienced professionals, often at the executive level, can find career opportunities that best match their skills and expertise. Seasoned executives using

---

50   https://www.myersbriggs.org/my-mbti-personality-type/take-the-mbti -instrument/
51   https://www.assessment.com/
52   https://www.enneagraminstitute.com/rheti
53   http://gamechangers.co/
54   https://www.forbes.com/sites/skollworldforum/2013/11/04/gamechangers -the-worlds-top-purpose-driven-organizations/#5ceea5ef77b6
55   https://80000hours.org
56   https://80000hours.org/job-board/
57   https://www.headhunter.com/

this site no longer have to search through non-relevant positions (e.g., entry level) to discover a job opening that matches them.

- **Idealist**[58] – the listings are job vacancies, internships, and volunteer positions in non-profit organizations.

- **LinkedIn**[59] – although it is not officially a jobs listing website, LinkedIn is a social media platform used by professionals to network with others and offers opportunities to link you with businesses that might have a vacancy in your field of expertise. It is a great way to build connections, and you might find the perfect job match through referrals from other professionals in your network.

- **Glassdoor**[60] – This is a jobs and recruiting site that provides a database (pay, work environment, company culture, etc.) about companies in different sectors. The info usually comes from employees (current and former) and from people who have gone through the interview process.

- **CareerBuilder**[61] – Created in 1995, CareerBuilder is one of the oldest job boards and has postings from all across the globe.

Option 2: Find Purpose outside of Your Job

The simple truth is many people *hate* their job, but they don't hate it enough to change careers. Instead, they'd rather look for purpose and meaning outside of their 9-to-5 grind. If that

---

58   https://www.idealist.org
59   https://www.linkedin.com/
60   https://www.glassdoor.com
61   https://www.careerbuilder.com/

sounds like you, I suggest you ask yourself a series of important questions like:

- What difference can I make to give others a better life? *Finding yourself is good, but losing yourself to something larger and more encompassing is truly awesome.*

- What am I willing to go the extra mile for? *The sense of fulfillment calls for you to make an effort, experience failure, yet have another go, and learn from experience.*

- What makes me forget about the passage of time? *Think of the activities that you do wherein you forget everything else, even sleeping and eating, because you were so immersed in what psychologists call the "flow" and the spirituals call tapping into the Divine.*

- Think back to when you were eight years old, and ask yourself: *What did I love to do? What activities did I do just for the sheer fun of it?*

- What am I willing to do despite looking like an idiot? *When you could care less about other people's opinions about you, you're training yourself to go after things that you feel are important, that are meaningful to you. Regardless if others don't share your sentiments.*

- If I only had a year left to live, how would I spend those 365 days? *Thinking about death, your own death, forces you to focus on what's truly important. Having a purpose in life means knowing exactly what's important to you.*

- When people come to me for help, what do they usually ask me to do?

- What things abilities, skills, and/or talents do I have?

- If I were given an opportunity to teach young people, what would I teach them?
- When do I feel most real?
- What do people usually thank me for?
- If I were given the chance to no longer work for a living but do something I truly love, what would that be?
- Complete this sentence: I wish _____.

Sure, you might not be able to find a job that fulfills the answers to these questions. But maybe you can find meaning by volunteering with an organization, starting a side hustle, or focusing on a hobby that you love. If any of these suggestions sound appetizing, I recommend you read (and implement) the strategies covered in the book *Designing Your Life*[62] by Bill Burnett and Dave Evans.

---

62   https://www.amazon.com/Designing-Your-Life-Well-Lived-Joyful/dp/1101875321/

4. Socialize with the *Right* People

Say yes instead of no. Turn off the TV and go make new friends. Finish reading the book or blog post later. Go to Meetup.com[63] and try something new.

The truth is: Engaging in a fun social activity can be one of the most pleasurable experiences available to humankind.

Even for introverts like myself, our current state of social inactivity is unnatural and unhealthy. In one study,[64] folks were randomly pinged through the day and asked what they were doing and how they felt. Out of the more than two dozen most common activities, social activity was reported on average as highly pleasurable, second only to sex.

In another study,[65] those who were the happiest spent 25% less time alone and 70% more time talking than the unhappiest participants.

Specifically, the unhappiest spent 76.8% of their time alone, while the happiest spent 58.6% by themselves. This was calculated by attaching discrete audio recorders to participants and seeing what percentage of the time they were silent or part of a conversation.

There are several factors at play that cause us, myself included, to choose TV and Internet over socializing, even though socializing brings more happiness.

---

63   http://www.meetup.com/
64   https://pdfs.semanticscholar.org/9dcf/d877e39b7b2f0e56bd468030081ca0a435e3.pdf
65   https://www.sciencedaily.com/releases/2010/03/100304165902.htm

TV and Internet appeal strongly to our desire for novelty. There's always something new going on. This is true with social contact too—no two conversations are ever the same. The difference is that social activity requires effort, while watching TV and using the Internet don't. In an ancestral environment, information was like sugar—rare and valuable. In the modern world, information is also like sugar—abundant and more junk than value.

Furthermore, emotions are contagious.[66] Scientists are still debating the how and why, but we all know this intuitively. When we talk to someone sad, we tend to get depressed ourselves. When we talk to someone filled with joy, we just can't help but feel a little better.

A long-term network study of 4,739 connected individuals[67] put numbers to our intuition:

You are 15% more likely to be happy if a directly connected friend is happy, 9.8% more likely if a friend of a friend is happy, and 5.6% if a friend of a friend of a friend is happy.

That's right—a friend of a friend of a friend, someone you don't even know, has more influence on your happiness than the size of your TV.

This was shown to be true after controlling for all sorts of confounding factors. Your friend of a friend of a friend actually influences your friend's friend, who in turn influences your friend, who influences you.

That being said, the key to making this strategy work is to socialize with the *right* people.

---

66 http://en.wikipedia.org/wiki/Emotional_contagion
67 https://www.bmj.com/content/337/bmj.a2338

In other words, you should spend less time with negative people. But you've probably heard that before. Instead, I suggest that you spend more time with happy people.

Happiness is more contagious than unhappiness.

Each additional happy friend that you have increases the chance of you being happy by 9%. Each additional unhappy friend increases the chance of you being unhappy by 7%.

One happy friend more than cancels out an unhappy one. The good news for happy people is that we are more likely to become friends with those who are similar to us. Happy people tend to marry each other, the same way that unhappy people tend to marry each other. It's a self-reinforcing cycle, good for those born lucky. What can the rest of us do?

To implement this idea, I recommend two simple rules:

1. Make an effort to befriend the happier people in your life.

Think of one person in your life who is full of positivity but who you aren't close with. Make the effort to change that—it will be worth it.

With these people, I recommend you:

- Make time for regular check-ins with friends. Strengthen your bond with very close friends through twice-weekly[68] phone calls.

- Be with them to celebrate milestones and joyous occasions in their lives. Call/meet with them for birthdays, holidays,

---

68   https://thelede.blogs.nytimes.com/2008/04/22/a-simple-bff-strategy -confirmed-by-scientists/?_r=0

and major personal achievements. The more you help celebrate the milestones of the important people in your life, the happier *you* will feel.

- Be an active and mindful[69] listener; that is, give comments as appropriate and not just the automatic, "Uh-huh, that's great to hear!" Results of several studies show that people love to talk about themselves—and love to hear themselves talk.

If you want a social circle full of vibrancy, however, you'll also need to follow the second step:

2. Make an effort to find happy people you can befriend.

Luckily, the best way to find and make friends with happy people is to do the things they do. The things they do are often great happiness-boosters in and of themselves. Here are a few options:

- **Yoga.** Yoga improves mood much more than other types of exercise that would burn the same number of calories.

- **Meditation.** Practicing meditation is one of the most effective ways to permanently boost mood, aside from getting kissed by Megan Fox.

- **Going to church.** I'm not religious, but I can tell you that if I were, I would love the sense of community and higher purpose found in church. Frequent churchgoers are, on average, 10% happier than their less religious peers.

- **Getting a pet.** There is a significant positive correlation between mood and the number of interactions with pets.

- **Going to the gym or joining a sports team, the local pick-up**

---

69   https://www.developgoodhabits.com/mindful-listening/

game, or the running club. People who exercise are happier than people who don't.

- **Create a group by introducing two people to each other.** This may seem farfetched, but if the individuals you introduce to each other hit it off nicely, you'll be sure that you will be part of the activity if they want to hang out. You'll now be a group.[70] Then introduce another person. Then another. To ensure that everybody sticks to the group, you must introduce people who seem likely to have common interests and temperaments as the others.

- **Be a volunteer.** Strong friendships usually form when people work together for a common cause or mutual interest.

- **Talk to strangers.** When the opportunity presents itself, muster the courage to start a conversation with someone while following social prompts.

- **Participate in meetups.** There are whole worlds on the Internet dedicated to groups sharing common interests. And these groups usually arrange face-to-face meetups of members located in the same geographical area. Join one and see how it goes meeting people who are interested in the same things you are.

- **Spend more time with an acquaintance.** Think about people you've spoken with in passing and find interesting. They could be friends of friends you're interested to know better because you find them engaging. Perhaps, like you, people you're acquainted with are uncertain of how to expand

---

70   https://getthefriendsyouwant.com/how-to-build-a-social-circle-from -scratch/

their social circle but are interested in becoming friends. Try reaching out and inviting them to hang out.

Go to events. Every major city regularly offers events in the form of concerts, exhibits, or festivals. Go to an event where you're likely to meet people your age, and grab the opportunity to meet like-minded people.

Picking just one of these activities can have a doubly tremendous impact on your mood: once because of the activity itself, and a second time because you'll be meeting and bonding with happy people.

More Information

- Social Time Crucial to Daily Emotional Wellbeing in U.S.[71]
- How to Be Happy[72]
- Eavesdropping on Happiness: Well-Being Is Related to Having Less Small Talk and More Substantive Conversations[73]
- A Survey Method for Characterizing Daily Life Experience: The Day Reconstruction Method[74]
- Looking to happy tomorrows with friends: Best and close friendships as they predict happiness[75]

---

71   http://www.gallup.com/poll/107692/social-time-crucial-daily-emotional-wellbeing.aspx

72   http://lesswrong.com/lw/4su/how_to_be_happy/

73   https://www.ncbi.nlm.nih.gov/pmc/articles/PMC2861779/

74   https://pdfs.semanticscholar.org/9dcf/d877e39b7b2f0e56bd468030081ca0a435e3.pdf

75   http://link.springer.com/article/10.1007/s10902-006-9025-2

5. Get Regular Exercise

Cardio, strength training, or high-intensity training—whatever your preference, make the commitment to get regular exercise. Not for the sake of your health or your appearance, but for happiness.

Getting regular exercise increases happiness just as much as doubling one's income would.

Exercise is at the top of this list, and for a reason—it's a wonder drug.

If you've been inactive, regular exercise will boost your long-term well-being by 10–15%.

In one study,[76] after eight weeks of exercising for 30 minutes three times a week, folks reported a 12% increase in their well-being.

There are a number of additional studies confirming the powerful results of exercise, as well as a number of different explanations for why exercise is so powerful for improving mental health. In my own life, I found a dramatic increase in my mood and energy level after exercising regularly for a few weeks. After I upped the frequency and intensity, I experienced a sustained mood bump.

One study[77] found that exercise was just as effective as an anti-depressant for improving mood. More significantly, those in the exercise group were five times less likely to relapse than those given a drug.

---

76   https://digitalcommons.wayne.edu/cgi/viewcontent.cgi?article=1037&context=honorstheses

77   https://www.ncbi.nlm.nih.gov/pmc/articles/PMC3674785/

There are three different explanations for where those benefits are coming from: the mastery hypothesis, the distraction hypothesis, and the chemical hypothesis.

The *mastery hypothesis* suggests the increase in mood originates from the feelings of self-esteem and self-efficacy that come from our being able to push our bodies beyond our preconceived limits.

The *distraction hypothesis* suggests that exercise is like meditation—a forced break from the stresses of life.

The *chemical hypothesis* suggests that exercise releases chemicals that reduce stress and improve mental functioning. Personally, my bet is on this hypothesis. For example, exercise causes a drop in levels of stress hormones, like cortisol, causes a rise in levels of happiness hormones, like endorphins, and increases levels of brain-derived neuropathic growth factor, which improves the functioning of the brain.

One important caveat: you might feel worse at first. Many who are inactive but decide to start exercising feel worse during their first few sessions. Don't worry, the dip is temporary and will soon be reversed!

Now, I'll be the first to admit that the idea of exercising every day *doesn't* sound like a happy experience. So my suggestion is to focus on a simple strategy that isn't painful and doesn't require too much of your free time. One great option is to create a walking habit where you aim for a minimum of 5,000 to 10,000 steps per day.

Here's how to turn walking into a habit:

First, you should purchase and wear a step-tracking device. If you're not familiar with them, step trackers are small devices or watches that track your total steps and floors climbed every day.

If you don't have a step tracker, check out the exhaustive review on my blog,[78] which compares the pricing and features of popular pedometers.

Next, make the commitment to put on this device each morning. At first glance, this might seem like an inconsequential habit. But there are a surprising number of people who buy these devices and never wear them. If *you* start each day by clipping on this device, you'll take that crucial first step to building the walking habit. And when you constantly wear this device, you'll find reasons to get more movement throughout the day.

Third, walk for five minutes every hour. While some people (like me) prefer a scheduled time of day to get exercise, others find it's better to walk throughout their workday, specifically between blocks of focused effort.

For instance, if you have a job that requires you to sit at a desk all day, you can set an alarm every hour to remind you to get up and walk around for five minutes.

Finally, look for "extra steps" throughout the day. You'd be amazed at how many steps you can rack up just by doing a few little things each day. Consider this list of ways to get extra steps during your day:

- Whenever you have a meeting of some kind, pace while you wait for it to start. This also applies in the doctor's office, in line at the Department of Motor Vehicles, or even in the pickup line at your kids' school. Even if you only pace for

---

78   https://www.developgoodhabits.com/pedometer-reviews/

two to three minutes, it adds up to 240 to 360 steps at 120 steps per minute.

- When you go shopping and aren't in a hurry, do a lap or two around the farthest aisles. Or, if you prefer, just walk up and down every aisle again, which has the added benefit of letting you check for specials you may have missed the first time around.

- At work, instead of using the closest restroom, travel one floor up or one floor down. Be sure to use the stairs to do so.

- Get up to change the channel on the TV or the CD in the player. Adjust your computer-run music player manually instead of using the remote. Walk around the house instead of relying on anything automated. Do the dishes by hand instead of using the dishwasher. Be creative around the house.

- If you're responsible for driving the kids to various activities, take a walk or two around the block while the activity is going on. You can still watch a baseball game while walking around the field, for example.

- If you take mass transit to work, get off a stop or two early. If you're particularly brave, set out even earlier and walk all the way to work.

- Start doing yard work yourself instead of hiring someone to do it. Walk around the house after completing each task instead of just going to the next job.

- If all you need are a couple of items, walk to the grocery store and back instead of driving. Put this one together with the second idea in this list to get a double boost.

- Make walking a family outing after dinner. Not only will this create quality bonding time with your family, but it'll also serve as an example to them of the benefits of walking.

- Instead of sitting down to talk on the phone, wander around the house, especially up and down stairs.

- Get your coworkers involved. The next time there's a meeting, take a walk outside in the nice weather and have the meeting while walking.

- Avoid escalators and elevators if doing so won't make you unduly late.

- If you're stuck at a desk for work, set your computer's alarm to go off every two hours. Get up each time it beeps, and walk down the hall or around the office. Chances are, you'll have to talk to someone on these trips anyway, so you'll not only increase your number of steps but also your productivity.

- If you're in a relationship, go out for dinner and then take a romantic walk afterward to start burning off the calories.

- Get up early and walk to a scenic location to see the sunrise or take a late walk to catch the sunset. Combine this one with the previous tip and make it a picnic instead of going out for dinner.

- If you go to church, invite a couple of people from the next pew to go for a walk afterward instead of hanging around for coffee hour.

- If you like tag sales, walk around the neighborhood instead of driving to find those deals. If you can't carry what you buy, the person will likely hold it for you while you dash home for your vehicle.

- If you're an animal lover, go to your local animal shelter and volunteer to walk dogs.

- If you want to meet a friend for coffee, walk to your favorite place. Invite your friend to go walking with you.

- If you live near a mall, get up early and go walk laps with the "mall walkers club."

As you can see, there are many simple ways to add walking as a simple exercise habit. And you'll find that the more you're moving, the more you'll experience a surge of those happy endorphins.

More Information

- Visua.ly, The Happiness Effect[79]

- What Happens to Our Brains When We Exercise and How It Makes Us Happier[80]

- How Exercise Benefits the Brain[81]

- Strength Training Effects on Subjective Well-Being and Physical Function in the Elderly[82]

- Physical Exercise and Psychological Well-Being: A Population Study in Finland[83]

- Physical Exercise and Depression[84]

79   http://visual.ly/happiness-effect-how-exercise-makes-you-happy
80   http://blog.bufferapp.com/why-exercising-makes-us-happier
81   http://well.blogs.nytimes.com/2011/11/30/how-exercise-benefits-the -brain/?_r=1&
82   https://journals.humankinetics.com/doi/abs/10.1123/japa.4.1.56
83   http://www.sciencedirect.com/science/article/pii/S0091743599905972
84   https://www.ncbi.nlm.nih.gov/pmc/articles/PMC474733/

- Moderators of the Relationship between Exercise and Mood Changes: Gender, Exertion Level, and Workout Duration[85]
- Getting Off the Hedonic Treadmill, One Step at a Time: The Impact of Regular Religious Practice and Exercise on Well-Being[86]

---

85 http://libres.uncg.edu/ir/asu/f/Rocheleau_Courtney_2004_Moderators_of _the_Relationship.pdf

86 https://www.hbs.edu/faculty/Pages/item.aspx?num=34716

6. Get Outside

One of the major advantages of building a walking habit is you're probably spending more time outdoors, which is another major lever of increasing happiness.

In fact, it's been said that happiness is **maximized at 57 degrees**.

The American Meteorological Society[87] published research in 2011 that found current temperature has a bigger effect on our happiness than variables like wind speed and humidity, or even the average temperature over the course of a day. It also found that **happiness is maximized at 57°F (13.9°C)**, so keep an eye on the weather forecast before heading outside for your 20 minutes of fresh air.

Furthermore, in *The Happiness Advantage*,[88] Shawn Achor recommends spending time in the fresh air to improve your happiness:

> Making time to go outside on a nice day also delivers a huge advantage; one study found that spending 20 minutes outside in good weather not only boosted positive mood, but broadened thinking and improved working memory.

This is pretty good news for those of us who are worried about fitting new habits into our already-busy schedules. That 20 minutes is a short enough time to spend outside that you could fit it into your commute or even your lunch break.

---

87 http://journals.ametsoc.org/doi/abs/10.1175/WCAS-D-11-00052.1?journalCode=wcas

88 http://www.amazon.com/gp/product/0307591549/ref=as_li_ss_tl?ie=UTF8&tag=spacforrent-20&linkCode=as2&camp=1789&creative=390957&creativeASIN=0307591549

In another study, the London School of Economics and Political Science conducted pioneering research[89] into the relationship between the environment and people's well-being.

Using an app called *Mappiness*,[90] 22,000 participants were asked to log their emotional states at regular points throughout the day. The study discovered a positive relationship between a person's well-being or sense of happiness and his/her exposure to natural or green surroundings.

In other words, the times people showed significantly higher happiness levels were those they spent outdoors in natural environments compared with time spent in urban settings.

Finally, in a recent pilot program called "Nature Prescriptions" that was rolled out last year in Shetland, UK,[91] doctors promoted spending time in nature for their patients.

They found numerous positive benefits to spending time in nature, like lowering hypertension, decreasing feelings of anxiety, and increasing feelings of happiness. The program recognizes that people are becoming increasingly disconnected from nature.

If any of these studies has convinced you about the advantages of getting outdoors more, here is a list of ways to add more nature to your life:

- Gather mushrooms or pick berries in the forest.
- Take a hike through a forest or in a city park.

89   https://www.parisschoolofeconomics.eu/IMG/pdf/Mackerron_paper.pdf
90   https://www.mappinessapp.com/
91   https://edition.cnn.com/2018/10/05/health/nature-prescriptions-shetland-intl/index.html

- Walk the dog in the park. Don't have a dog? Make a friend happy by being a dog sitter for the day.

- Forest bathe.[92]

- Bike (cross country, downhill, or trail).

- Spend a day at the beach or other body of water. Scientists are finding[93] that bodies of water, such as oceans and lakes, have restorative powers. Regardless of the reason, there's no question that we feel better after a day at the beach.

- Go river rafting.[94]

- Go camping with friends or family.

- Try solo backpacking.[95]

- Spend your weekend reading, writing, sketching, or lounging at the park. Do not take your phone.

- Go outside regardless of the weather—enjoy the rain, wind, snow, or sunshine on your face.

- Grow a garden in your backyard.

- Go cloud watching.

- Draw stick figures (or any artistic masterpiece) in the sand.

- Jump in a puddle.

- Make some daisy chains.

- Blow a dandelion. Be sure to make a wish first.

- Identify the bird species in the park nearest your home.

---

92   https://www.growwilduk.com/blog/2015/12/03/5-simple-steps-practising-shinrin-yoku-forest-bathing

93   http://barryyeoman.com/2013/02/beach-happiness-neuroconservation/

94   https://www.riverrunnersusa.com/stories-from-the-river/2017/7/16/five-ways-rafting-can-help-you-unwind

95   https://travelhappy.info/travel-tips/seven-reasons-to-go-travelling-solo/

- Go on a treasure hunt. Try geocaching.[96]
- Write a poem in the woods.
- Do yoga in the forest or near a body of water.
- Listen to the song of birds.
- If you can't get out, tend a houseplant.
- Have a picnic for your family.
- Breathe in the aromas of nature.
- Listen to the ocean waves.

---

96 https://www.geocaching.com/play

7. Get a Full Night's Rest

Spend more time sleeping. Go to sleep at approximately the same time every day. Avoid caffeine in the evening. Don't stay in bed if you can't sleep. Avoid TV and Internet in the 20 minutes before sleep. You know what I'm talking about. Those who report getting less and worse quality sleep also report having lower life satisfaction.

Gretchen Rubin says it best in her book *The Happiness Project*:[97]

> Getting one extra hour of sleep each night would do more for your daily happiness than getting a $60,000 raise.

The allure to stay awake is huge, though, isn't it? There's just so much more to do—watch another episode of *Game of Thrones*, read another book or blog post, answer a few more emails. The problem is that for now, it takes seven to nine hours of quality sleep to maximize health and well-being.

The link between happiness and sleep is complex but strong. Those who have more and better sleep report higher life satisfaction and happiness. Those who have less and poorer sleep are several times more likely to develop depression.

Depriving yourself of sleep during the weekdays then catching up on weekends isn't harmless. Likewise, for most folks with insomnia, their baseline level of happiness has gradually shifted to a significantly lower level.

Of course, getting more high-quality sleep isn't as easy as adding flossing to your routine. Think of it like a long-term project.

---

97   https://www.amazon.com/dp/B07CRQMQ17/ref=dp-kindle-redirect ?_encoding=UTF8&btkr=1

If you're someone who has trouble getting to bed early, here are nine strategies that can help:

1. **Use soothing sounds.** There is a reason lullabies put babies to sleep. The mind and body desire rest when they hear restful and peaceful sounds. Soothing music, a white noise generator, or even simple earplugs will provide the soothing sounds you need to fall asleep.

2. **Expend energy during the day.** If you are exhausted from physical exercise, it is far easier to sleep at night. A workout just before bedtime, however, is counterproductive, so plan accordingly.

3. **Cut out caffeine and cigarettes before sleep.** These interfere with getting to sleep and can make you feel "wired" throughout the evening. Generally speaking, it's recommended you avoid these substances *at least* three hours before bedtime.

4. **Imagine a relaxing scene.** Picture yourself sitting on a beach, walking a garden path, or getting a relaxing massage. It's much easier to fall asleep to calming visualizations than to worries about what's going on in your life.

5. **Avoid excessive screen time right before sleeping**. Studies have shown[98] that back-lit screen use (television, computers, and cell phones) at night can lead to sleep disorders. It is far better to do a bit of paperwork, read a book, or just unwind with your loved ones before going to sleep.

6. **Make your bedroom for sleeping.** Keep the modern distractions out. Get rid of the television, computer, and other

---

98   http://www.huffingtonpost.com/david-volpi-md-pc-facs/technology-depression_b_1723625.html

electronics in your bedroom. Make it a place to get your full night's rest.

7. **Adjust the temperature.** Like Goldilocks, you want your bedroom temp to be "just right." Your bedroom should be cool, but not cold, to help promote sleep.

8. **Create a comfortable sleep environment.** Keep your sheets fresh and laundered. Make sure your pillow is comfortable. You spend a third of your life in bed, so do it in style and comfort.

9. **Practice deep breathing.** Take long, deep breaths. Inhale slowly. Exhale slowly. Think of the relaxing scene from tip 4.

Getting a full night's sleep isn't that hard if you make it a priority. If you implement these nine actions, you'll find it's easier to get to bed earlier and wake up feeling a little bit happier.

More Information

- A Fundamental Secret to Happiness? Get Enough Sleep.[99]
- From a Sleep Study, Clues to Happiness[100]
- How Much Sleep Do We Really Need?[101]
- How artificial light is wrecking your sleep, and what to do about it[102]

---

99   http://www.psychologytoday.com/blog/the-happiness-project/200911/fundamental-secret-happiness-get-enough-sleep

100   http://well.blogs.nytimes.com/2013/03/21/from-a-sleep-study-clues-to-happiness/?_r=0&gwh=0942E8A8A0E02C65146A6FE72645F385

101   http://sleepfoundation.org/how-sleep-works/how-much-sleep-do-we-really-need

102   http://chriskresser.com/how-artificial-light-is-wrecking-your-sleep-and-what-to-do-about-it

- The Associations Between Life Satisfaction and Health-related Quality of Life, Chronic Illness, and Health Behaviors among U.S. Community-dwelling Adults[103]

- Sleep-Length and Life Satisfaction in a College Student Sample[104]

- Annual Sleep in America Poll Exploring Connections with Communications Technology Use and Sleep[105]

- Action Spectrum for Melatonin Regulation in Humans: Evidence for a Novel Circadian Photoreceptor[106]

- Epidemiology of insomnia, depression, and anxiety[107]

- Depression and Insomnia[108]

- The Link between Sleep and Mood[109]

- Cumulative Sleepiness, Mood Disturbance, and Psychomotor Vigilance Performance Decrements during a Week of Sleep Restricted to 4-5 Hours per Night[110]

103   http://link.springer.com/article/10.1007/s10900-007-9066-4#page-1

104   https://eric.ed.gov/?id=EJ706691

105   http://www.sleepfoundation.org/article/press-release/annual-sleep-america-poll-exploring-connections-communications-technology-use-

106   http://www.jneurosci.org/content/21/16/6405.abstract

107   http://www.ncbi.nlm.nih.gov/pubmed?Db=pubmed&Cmd=ShowDetailView&TermToSearch=16335332&ordinalpos=9&itool=EntrezSystem2.PEntrez.Pubmed.Pubmed_ResultsPanel.Pubmed_RVDocSum

108   http://www.webmd.com/depression/features/sleep-problems

109   http://healthysleep.med.harvard.edu/need-sleep/whats-in-it-for-you/mood

110   http://www.ncbi.nlm.nih.gov/pubmed/9231952

8. Help Others and Volunteer

Mentor students. Serve food to the homeless. Collect money. Read to underserved kids. Clean up the local park. Visit the elderly. Walk shelter dogs. Volunteer.

Volunteer—not because you want to help others but because you want to help yourself.

There are many reasons volunteering is beneficial: It gives us a sense of meaning. It increases our social activity. It introduces us to novel and potentially exciting activities. And because volunteering gives us an opportunity to demonstrably improve the world, it increases our self-esteem.

Put together, this is the reason volunteering increases well-being, life-satisfaction, and reduces mortality risk in older adults.

One important caveat is that folks who are happier are themselves more likely to volunteer. So, although folks who volunteer are more likely to be happy, some of that difference is because folks who are already happier for other reasons are more likely to volunteer.

Here are three tips to keep in mind when choosing the type of volunteer activities you try:

1. In one study,[111] authors tried to figure out what factors predicted whether volunteers would quit or continue. The two most predictive factors were *engagement* and *meaning*. When you are volunteering, does time fly by, and do you

---

111   http://www.asanet.org/sites/default/files/savvy/images/members/docs/pdf /featured/volunteer.pdf

think your contributions are making the world a better place?

2. One of the biggest benefits of volunteering can be found when it's done with a group. It also helps when you get to see the benefits of your actions.

3. For the men reading this, "altruism" is a courtship display. In one study,[112] 300 women were shown dating profiles. Those profiles that included volunteering were more likely to be rated highly. Not only does volunteering demonstrate generosity over selfishness, it's also a signal that you're more likely to be happy, healthy, and have a stronger social network.

Now, one of the biggest barriers to volunteering is uncertainty. You might want to help, but you're unsure about how much time it requires or where to get started. By scheduling an activity in advance, you'll eliminate any excuse for not helping others.

There are a few ways to find volunteering opportunities in your immediate area. First, most local libraries and community centers post flyers and advertisements for organizations that need help. If you can't find any, ask a staff member where you can find information about different activities coming up.

The Internet is also a good option for finding volunteer opportunities. There are three websites I would recommend:

*   http://www.volunteermatch.org
*   http://www.idealist.org/
*   http://www.pointsoflight.org/handsonnetwork

The first two websites are similar to one another. You can search

112   http://news.bbc.co.uk/2/hi/health/8505641.stm

your area by the type of organization you're looking for or do a search based on a specific skill. The third website only has the option to search by the type of organization you'd like to help.

Finally, you can work with your local church to find volunteering opportunities. Most faith-based groups regularly organize activities where members help others while spreading the word about their religion. You can find information on these activities by attending a service and checking out the weekly bulletin.

It's not hard to find volunteering opportunities in your area. Instead of doing it at the last minute, set aside time each week to find and schedule an activity.

More Information

- Volunteering Makes You Happier[113]
- Volunteering Could Boost Happiness, Decrease Depression And Help You Live Longer: Study[114]
- Dating study: women prefer "men who are kind"[115]
- Effects of Volunteering on the Well-Being of Older Adults[116]
- Formal Volunteering as a Protective Factor for Older Adults' Psychological Well-Being[117]
- Volunteer Work and Well-Being[118]

---

113   http://www.fastcoexist.com/3016549/volunteering-makes-you-happier

114   http://www.huffingtonpost.com/2013/08/23/volunteering-happiness
-depression-live-longer_n_3804274.html

115   http://news.bbc.co.uk/2/hi/health/8505641.stm

116   https://academic.oup.com/psychsocgerontology/article/58/3/S137
/583366

117   http://www.midus.wisc.edu/findings/pdfs/147.pdf

118   http://oarhmlh.asanet.org/images/members/docs/pdf/featured/volunteer
.pdf

9. Keep a Gratitude Journal

Once a day, take a few moments to write down or verbalize three things that happened that make you feel grateful.

In fact, you can break it down into a simple exercise:

"Write down three things that went well that day and their causes every night. In addition, provide a causal explanation for each good thing."

That's it! We spend tens of thousands of dollars on expensive electronics, homes, automobiles, and vacations hoping for a 10% boost. There is a free alternative, and it works.

In a study[119] of this exercise's effectiveness by Martin Seligman, participants were asked to follow those exact instructions for just one week.

After one week they were 2% happier than before, but in follow-up tests, their happiness kept on increasing, from 5% at one month, to 9% at six months. All this, even though they were only instructed to journal for one week. Participants enjoyed the exercise so much, they just kept on doing it on their own.

How can a gratitude journal make us so much happier?

Three reasons:

First, the brain is like a muscle. Every time you practice gratitude, you're exercising the neural pathways responsible for finding reasons to be happy.

Second, the actual gratitude produced during those five minutes

---

119   https://www.ncbi.nlm.nih.gov/pubmed/16045394

is small, but the emotions of gratitude felt during those five-minutes can be enough to trigger a grateful mood.

While in a grateful mood, further feelings of gratitude are more likely to trigger, even on their own, without conscious direction.

Third, and most importantly, because of hedonic adaptation, we get used to the good things in our life.

It makes sense that we get tired of our old car and of our old wife. From an evolutionary perspective, it's good to upgrade to a new model; it's good to get more food, build bigger houses, and construct pointier weapons. **But it sucks for our happiness.**

Remember the last time you bought yourself a nice toy? It could be a game, a car, a TV, a piece of clothing … anything you bought because you expected it to give you happiness. It probably made you happy, but for how long? More specifically, when did it make you happy?

Your material good made you happy when you were consciously thinking about it. Taking the example of a TV, the first few times you sat down to watch it, you actually thought about the features of the TV. You might have thought, *The quality is so much better than that old piece of junk I had*, or, *I'm so glad I bought it—the size is great*. Whatever it was you thought, there was some form of appreciation. **Appreciation creates happiness.** It happened automatically.

And then it stopped. There was no more recognition—there were no more conscious thoughts. It became a part of your reality, undeserving of your mental time. With that change, you lost its happiness, forcing you to seek out the next toy.

We already have all the toys we need.

That said, you can counteract hedonic adaptation by regularly completing the "Three Good Things" exercise I mentioned at the beginning of this habit. By taking the time to consciously express gratitude, we remember that we already have many things we should be grateful and happy for. **Doing this exercise actually feels good.**

To get started, I recommend buying an inexpensive journal and using it to write down three things you're thankful for each day. Or you can check out a physical journal that I recently published, *The 90-Day Gratitude Journal: A Mindful Practice for a Lifetime of Happiness.*[120]

More Information

- The 31 Benefits of Gratitude You Didn't Know About: How Gratitude Can Change Your Life[121]

- Positive Psychology Progress[122]

- Counting Blessings Versus Burdens: An Experimental Investigation of Gratitude and Subjective Well-Being in Daily Life[123]

- Why Gratitude Enhances Well-Being: What We Know, What We Need to Know[124]

---

120   https://www.amazon.com/dp/1946159158

121   http://happierhuman.com/benefits-of-gratitude/

122   https://www.happierhuman.com/positive-psychology-progress-2005 -seligman-m-p-steen-t-a-park-n-peterson-c/

123   https://greatergood.berkeley.edu/images/application_uploads/Emmons -CountingBlessings.pdf

124   https://www.researchgate.net/publication/279869542_Why_Gratitude _Enhances_Well-Being

PART 3:

FINDING HAPPINESS WITH OTHERS

10. Go to a Place of Worship

Those who attend a place of worship (i.e., a church, synagogue, mosque, or monastery) at least once a week are twice as likely to report being very happy.

In a survey of Americans[125] between 1972 and 2008, 26% of those who didn't attend religious services reported being "very happy," compared to 48% of those who attend services more than weekly.

Why?

- The social support provided by a religious community is unmatched by all other modern institutions.
- Spirituality is highly correlated with increased feelings of gratitude, respect, and optimism.
- Religion provides purpose and meaning in life.

It's crazy—half of those who regularly go to a place of worship report being very happy, compared to just one-fourth of atheists and people who aren't religious.

The key difference is to actually go to a place of worship instead of telling yourself that "you're spiritual" without ever attending a service.

There are two benefits for attending a religious service that being spiritual alone doesn't provide—the most friendly and supportive social community with shared values you're likely to find anywhere, and weekly micro-doses of happiness.

---

125   https://pdfs.semanticscholar.org/5cb5/761c0935f19501d7dc107f296605 724ad00b.pdf

One study[126] asked participants how happy they were right before they entered the church, and again after they exited. The average person reported a 4% mood bump. More significantly, these mood bumps were large enough to cause a change to participants' baseline level of happiness.

For each week a person attended a service over the past month, baseline happiness increased by 3.5%. For each additional visit after the four times a month Sunday service, baseline happiness increased by a further 1%. So the average person who went to church four times a month reported being 14% happier; the average person who went 10 times reported being 20% happier.

Two other reasons attending a religious service increases happiness is:

1. Because doing so increases feelings of gratitude and optimism, both of which themselves increase happiness,

2. Because religion provides purpose and meaning to life.

Bottom line: the social support provided by a religious community is unmatched by all other modern institutions.

And it is likely to stay that way for decades, centuries, or more.

At a high level, the four components that make religious communities social capital generators are: **trust** (e.g., "being in a cathedral builds up my sense of trust in other people"), **bonding** (e.g., "being in the cathedral helps me to make friends"), **bridging** (e.g., "being in the cathedral helps me to meet new people and contribute to community life"), and **linking** (e.g.,

---

126   https://www.huffpost.com/entry/going-to-church-mood-positive
-emotions-well-being_n_1375707

"I have met important people through my involvement in the cathedral).

Each of those individual components can be found elsewhere, but never as strongly.

- The level of trust you have of others in your congregation will be much stronger than your trust of those at your book club or dinner parties.

- Bonding opportunities may exist at your workplace, but the primary function of work is to work, not bond.

- Volunteering can help you meet new people and contribute to community life; but in my experience, religious groups get more done, have more enthusiasm for their cause, and form stronger relationships with one another and those whom they meet.

- It's possible to network with community leaders or powerful bankers, but the interaction just isn't the same as when it's between two equals in church, under the eyes of God.

So if you're a spiritual person who would like to build up your social network, one of the first places you should look is your local house of worship.

More Information

- Going To Church Linked With Better Mood, Study Finds[127]
- Study: Happiness Is Having Friends at Church[128]

---

127 http://www.huffingtonpost.com/2012/03/25/going-to-church-mood
-positive-emotions-well-being_n_1375707.html
128 http://usatoday30.usatoday.com/yourlife/mind-soul/spirituality/2010-12
-07-happyreligion07_ST_N.htm

- Happiness and Religion—Getting the Benefits Outside the Cathedral[129]

- Getting off the hedonic treadmill, one step at a time: The impact of regular religious practice and exercise on well-being[130]

- The Religion Paradox: If Religion Makes People Happy, Why Are So Many Dropping Out?[131]

- Religiosity/Spirituality and Mortality[132]

---

129 http://happierhuman.com/spirituality/

130 http://people.duke.edu/~dandan/webfiles/PapersUpside/Religion%20Hedonic%20Treadmill.pdf

131 http://www.ncbi.nlm.nih.gov/pubmed/21806304

132 http://www.karger.com/Article/Fulltext/190791

11. Write a Gratitude Letter

Think of three reasons you're grateful for a friend or acquaintance. Then go up to them and share. Or think of someone who's made a large impact on your life. Write down all the ways they've helped you, as well as the resulting positive impact that help has had on your life. Then go read the letter to them.

Self-reliance can be counterproductive to happiness. Expressing your appreciation to others will bring joy—both to you and to the recipients. In addition, I've found those moments of sharing a gratitude letter to be some of the most vulnerable of my life. Vulnerability creates connection.

In one study,[133] those who wrote and then sent a gratitude letter experienced, on average, an immediate 10% increase in happiness. One month later, half of that bump remained.

Why does expressing our appreciation make us so much happier?

Americans interpret feelings of gratitude as weakness. In my experience, it's the other way around—feelings of gratitude make you vulnerable. Embracing vulnerability requires strength.

Feelings of happiness come in many different shapes: joy, sensual pleasure, love, compassion, and so on.

One of those shapes is gratitude. That is, genuine feelings of gratitude are interpreted by our brain as feelings of happiness.

So how do you actually write a gratitude letter?

---

133   http://greatergood.berkeley.edu/pdfs/GratitudePDFs/2Wood
-GratitudeWell-BeingReview.pdf

Simple:

First, set aside half an hour to pen the letter. Go somewhere quiet where you're not likely to be interrupted by others.

Then picture in your mind the recipient of the letter. Recall what the person did for you that you feel grateful for and how much they've helped. Think of specific actions instead of generalities here.

Third, begin writing by specifically addressing the person you're writing to. For example: "Dear_____". Address them in writing the way you do when you're face to face.

Then in the main portion of the letter, express your gratitude (Thank you ...; I'm so grateful you were ...; It meant the world to me that ...) and describe the specific things this person has contributed to your life.

You can use these prompts to help you get started:

- Did they help you out financially when you needed it the most?
- Have they given you a timely piece of advice?
- Did they do something that helped you see the world in a better light?
- Did they believe in you when others didn't?

You can also include a description of how you are now, especially if you are acknowledging their contribution in your life.

Next, mention the date or occasion you might see them again. Or let them know they are in your thoughts.

Finally, as you close out the letter, restate your gratitude, wish

97

them well, and end the letter with your respects ("Sincerely" is universally acceptable, but something warmer or more personal is okay for closer relationships). Sign your name and immediately send the letter.

Doesn't seem that hard, right?

You'll find that the more you express gratitude *to others*, the happier you'll become. In turn, this happiness can be spread to the people in your life who have made a difference. If you'd like to learn more about the power of this simple habit, I recommend checking out the Say It With Gratitude website[134] run by my friend Scott Colby.

More Information

- How a Simple 'Thank You' Changed the World: The 1-Week LYL Team Gratitude Challenge Begins Today![135]

- The 31 Benefits of Gratitude You Didn't Know About: How Gratitude Can Change Your Life[136]

- Gratitude and Well-being: A Review and Theoretical Integration[137]

134   https://sayitwithgratitude.com/
135   http://liveyourlegend.net/the-gratitude-challenge/
136   https://www.happierhuman.com/benefits-of-gratitude/
137   http://greatergood.berkeley.edu/pdfs/GratitudePDFs/2Wood
-GratitudeWell-BeingReview.pdf

12. Engage in Deep Conversations

Skip the small talk. Ask atypical questions. Be more receptive to strange or personal questions.

The happiest people have twice as many deep conversations as the unhappiest ... so ditch the small talk!

Whether it's because deep conversations facilitate bonding or because we all have an innate desire to talk about important things, there is a strong correlation between having meaningful conversations and feeling happy.

It's possible that the correlation runs the other way—that happy people are simply more likely to engage in deep conversation. However, I think it goes both ways: being happy makes you more likely to talk about important things, and talking about important things makes you happy.

The study from which this idea was born[138] was conducted in 2009. Researchers attached discrete audio recorders to the 79 participants for four days. Afterward, the researchers calculated the percentage of the time participants spent alone, talking, in deep conversations, and in small talk.

The happiest participants spent almost half of their social time in deep conversation. The unhappiest spent only 21.8% of their social time in deep conversation.

One of my friends has taken the results of this study to heart. Once a month, she organizes a conversation night. We come up with a list of meaningful topics we would like to discuss, break into pairs, and discuss a topic. Then we switch partners and

---

138   https://www.ncbi.nlm.nih.gov/pmc/articles/PMC2861779/

talk about another topic. Participation requires sharing parts of yourself usually kept hidden (e.g., you can't talk about what your greatest fears are without opening up).

Not only does having those conversations make me feel great, but I also feel I've learned more about some of the participants in two hours than in dozens of hours of small talk. If deep conversation doesn't come easily for you, I recommend thinking up ahead of time interesting questions you can ask in place of the typical questions: What do you do? Where did you grow up? What's your favorite color?

If you'd like to engage in deep conversations, here are 64 prompts to help you get started:

1. Imagine hosting the perfect dinner party. You can invite anyone who has ever lived. Who would you include on the guest list?

2. When did you last talk to yourself?

3. Name two ways in which you consider yourself lucky.

4. Name something you have always wanted to do, and explain why you haven't done it yet.

5. Imagine that your house or apartment catches fire. You can save only one object. What would it be?

6. Describe one of the happiest days of your life.

7. Imagine you are going to become a close friend of mine. What is the most important thing for me to know about you?

8. Describe one of your most embarrassing moments.

9. Describe a personal problem, and ask your conversation partner's advice on how best to handle it.

10. What makes your heart beat faster?

11. Where do your passions lie?

12. What would you want me to discover about you?

13. How relaxed are you right now?

14. What's something you've done or experienced that not many people know about?

15. What are three things you're grateful for that happened in the past month?

16. What makes you appreciate that you're alive?

17. What do you hold dear?

18. What is the best advice you've ever received? And did you take it?

19. What is the most important thing in a friendship?

20. Who's your personal hero?

21. What do you constantly think about?

22. What's the most expensive thing you've ever given to someone?

23. What has changed in your life?

24. What book has most influenced how you think/live?

25. If there was one person you'd like to have a conversation with for an entire day, who would it be and why?

26. Which is more valuable: common sense or intelligence?

27. What movie has had the greatest influence on your life, and why?

28. What three non-electronic, non-automatic items would you take if you were stuck on a deserted island?

29. What can you say about white lies?

30. What is the most significant thing you miss about being a kid?

31. When was the last time you cried, and why?

32. Would you rather have your heart broken or break someone's heart, and why?

33. What keeps you going in life?

34. What three things would you wish for if a genie were to grant them today?

35. Which is worse: failing at something or not trying something?

36. Are you a giver or a taker?

37. What role does fate play in your life?

38. What are your thoughts on the saying "It takes a village to raise a child"?

39. What piece of advice would you give to an alien visiting our planet?

40. What is your definition of happiness?

41. When can we say that someone is successful?

42. What would you want to tell your 14-year-old self?

43. What defines you?

44. At this point in your life, what gives you a sense of fulfillment?

45. Who influences you in your decisions?

46. Which are more important: old friends or new friends?

47. Who has the right to define what is good and what is evil?

48. Where does your strength lie?

49. Can you be truly happy without any money?

50. How do you know if the way you perceive the world is real?

51. How "in control" are you in your own life?

52. Do you believe in giving others a second chance, and why or why not?

53. What do you think happens to a person after death?

54. If you had a week to live, how would you live the remaining days?

55. If you could travel back through time, which period would you visit and why?

56. If people have already achieved enlightenment, what do you think should be their next step?

57. If you were granted the power to change one period in history, what would it be and why?

58. What is your best birthday memory?

59. How do you define love?

60. Which is more important: trust or love?

61. What are your thoughts on the saying "All is fair in love and war"?

62. Do you believe that humans have souls?

63. How do you define reality?

64. Do you think the world can really achieve peace without using violence?

More Information

- Happiness and Deep Conversations[139]
- Talk Deeply, Be Happy?[140]
- Want to be happier? Skip the small talk[141]
- Eavesdropping on Happiness: Well-Being Is Related to Having Less Small Talk and More Substantive Conversations[142]

---

139   http://www.huffingtonpost.com/tom-morris/happiness-and-deep-conver
_b_507148.html

140   http://well.blogs.nytimes.com/2010/03/17/talk-deeply-be-happy/?_r=0

141   http://blogs.discovermagazine.com/seriouslyscience/2013/09/26/want-to
-be-happier-skip-the-small-talk/#.UpAqRsRDutw

142   https://www.ncbi.nlm.nih.gov/pmc/articles/PMC2861779/

13. Share Your Successes

When something good happens, tell people. Sharing both the good and the bad are two paths to deepening a relationship. But people like being vicariously happy more than being vicariously depressed. If good things don't happen to you that often, remember that life is subjective.

Finding things to identify as good is a skill. Work on it by sharing successes as often as possible.

Conversationally, humans are lazy. When asked how they've been, humans are more likely to share what's top of mind, rather than what's most important or most likely to improve the conversation. Because of our biological programming, one of the things that is most likely to be top of mind is whatever is going wrong.

Complaining can be useful for soliciting support and validation but is rarely the most useful response to a situation. When you share your successes and the good things that have happened to you, so long as you aren't an arrogant jerk, you're raising the mood of the room.

Although we don't usually realize it, many good things are happening to us all the time.

Of course, the key here is to share your positive experiences in a humble manner without coming across like you're bragging.

Here are a few strategies that can help you do this:

- **Identify what it is you want to share about yourself.** (Oftentimes, we wish to share how we overcame adversity in order to achieve the success we're experiencing right now).

- **Pay attention to timing; it's essential.** Sharing too much too quickly puts people off. Furthermore, sharing too often also deters people from appreciating your story as a source of inspiration.

- **Share something inspiring.** And be open to telling your audience that you were awed by the experience you're sharing with them.

- **Have a sense of humor.** Channel your inner comic to share something memorable about you.

- **Allow someone to endorse you.** An endorsement, a referral, or a recommendation about your abilities has a huge impact on telling other people about you. You don't have to advertise yourself. People are usually more receptive to third-party information about your success.

- **Avoid the "humblebrag."** The humblebrag is the quickest way for people to dislike you.[143] You've probably seen posts like these on social media. These are the updates that are written to sound like a complaint, but they are a not-so-subtle way to tell people how awesome you think you are. For example: "I was wearing grubby clothes and my hair was a mess, but all these guys were *still* hitting on me today."

- **Be yourself.** If you had humble beginnings, telling people about that usually makes you a more memorable individual. Oftentimes, people remember us not for our impressive educational achievements or amazing work credentials. We make better impressions through the stories we share about our lives.

---

143   http://time.com/5095144/humblebrag-bragging/

14. Savor Those Small Moments

Many people rush through their day without noticing the world around them. They are so fixated on appointments, errands, to-do lists, and everything in between that they fail to savor the small moments. This chronic fixation is bad for happiness; it's a classic symptom of people who allow their monkey mind[144] to run wild. They are overwhelmed by chaotic thoughts that are often related to the same topics. This way of thinking leads to anxiety, insomnia, and even rage.

The solution to this negative tendency lies in mindfulness or, specifically, dispositional mindfulness.[145] It is becoming keenly aware of and attentive to your thoughts and feelings *right now*. Simply, it is the art of savoring the moment.

Scientists have recently been tracking the relationship between happiness and dispositional mindfulness. A study about dispositional mindfulness[146] reveals that aside from having numerous positive health benefits,[147] being mindful of one's thoughts and feelings in the present moment **predicts a healthy psyche**.

Another study[148] reveals that dispositional mindfulness reduces stress and encourages a person to perform more self-care

---

144   https://www.developgoodhabits.com/how-to-quiet-your-monkey-mind/
145   https://www.marksdailyapple.com/the-what-why-and-how-of
-dispositional-mindfulness/
146   https://www.researchgate.net/publication/315923255_Being
_Present_and_Enjoying_It_Dispositional_Mindfulness_and_Savoring_the
_Moment_Are_Distinct_Interactive_Predictors_of_Positive_Emotions_and
_Psychological_Health
147   https://www.marksdailyapple.com/the-what-why-and-how-of
-dispositional-mindfulness/
148   https://www.ncbi.nlm.nih.gov/pmc/articles/PMC4481049/

activities. At present, there is a branch of study called *savoring*.[149] Its focus is on being fully engaged in thoughts and actions to help increase a person's appreciation of good experiences and positive emotions, with the goal of intensifying and prolonging this state of positivity.

There are different ways to savor the moment; see the suggestions we've listed below. To develop the habit of savoring, choose one behavior and practice it for a week or two until it's integrated into your daily routine. Then choose another, and another.

- **Allow time to flow.** Lose track of time by totally immersing your attention in what you're doing

- **Engage all your senses.** Heighten your perception by using your senses—sight, touch, smell, hearing, and taste—focusing on elements you wish to amplify. For example, while listening to music, close your eyes and allow yourself to be fully enveloped by what you're hearing.

- **Congratulate yourself.** Honor your personal victories, however small they are. Celebrate what you have achieved. Through this honoring, the feeling of success lingers long after the moment has passed.

- **Share your positive feeling with others.** Telling someone close to you when you are feeling a positive emotion can help you stay in that emotional state for a prolonged period.

- **Acknowledge and express gratefulness for all that you've received.** Let those you care about know how much their presence in your life means to you. Another way of

---

149   https://en.wikipedia.org/wiki/Savoring

expressing gratefulness is to take a few moments before each meal to appreciate the food set before you.

Aside from these suggestions, develop mindfulness by taking up a meditation practice, such as walking meditation, yoga, or qigong. Practicing meditation can help you slow your pace and be more fully present.

Stay present in the moment, anticipate, reminisce, share the experience with others, and practice gratitude and counterfactual thinking. Indulge in moderation.

15. Spend Money on Others

Get a coffee for a coworker. Buy a no-reason-just-felt-like-it gift for your romantic partner. Buy an extra apple from the grocery store and give it to the next homeless person you see.

Spending money on others does more for our happiness than spending money on ourselves.

Harvard researchers ran an experiment,[150] asking: Would students become happier spending money on themselves or spending on others?

They first measured how happy the students were in the morning. Then the students were given either $5 or $20. Half the group was told to spend the money on themselves, while the other half was told to spend the money on others.

No surprise—both groups reported an increase in happiness. Who wouldn't, having been given free money? But the group that spent money on others reported a larger increase in happiness.

There are a number of other studies that suggest that spending on others (within reason!) creates more happiness than spending on oneself. For example, those who spend more of their year-end bonus on others report a larger, longer-lasting increase in well-being than those who spend more on themselves.

One reason this is true is that we sometimes underestimate the impact that social approval has on our levels of happiness. In one study,[151] participants were put under an fMRI while either

---

150   http://www.forbes.com/sites/hbsworkingknowledge/2013/08/21/to-buy
-happiness-spend-money-on-others/
151   https://www.ncbi.nlm.nih.gov/pmc/articles/PMC4441506/

experiencing social rejection or social approval. Those experiencing social rejection were seen to activate some of the brain circuits involved with real, physical pain. Likewise, those experiencing social approval were seen to activate some of the brain circuits involved with real, physical pleasure.

So if you'd like to feel a quick jolt of happiness, look for small ways to spend money on the important people in your life.

More Information

- To Buy Happiness, Spend Money on Other People[152]
- How to Buy Happiness[153]
- Why Spending Money on Others Promotes Your Happiness[154]
- Money Can Buy Happiness If You Spend It On Others, Michael Norton Says[155]
- There's More to Life Than Happiness—But That Doesn't Make Wanting It Stupid or Selfish[156]
- Spending Money on Others Promotes Happiness[157]
- Prosocial Spending and Well-Being: Cross-Cultural Evidence for a Psychological Universal[158]
- The Psychological Consequences of Money[159]

152   http://www.forbes.com/sites/hbsworkingknowledge/2013/08/21/to-buy
-happiness-spend-money-on-others/
153   http://www.youtube.com/watch?v=PsihkFWDt3Y
154   http://www.spring.org.uk/2011/10/why-spending-money-on-others
-promotes-your-happiness.php
155   http://www.huffingtonpost.com/2012/05/01/money-can-buy-happiness
_n_1467789.html
156   http://happierhuman.com/happiness-is-not-hedonism/
157   http://www.people.hbs.edu/mnorton/dunn aknin norton.pdf
158   http://econpapers.repec.org/paper/nbrnberwo/16415.htm
159   http://www.sciencemag.org/content/314/5802/1154

16. Spend Money on Experiences

We just covered the importance of spending money on others, but one of the simplest ways to do this is to share great experiences with the people in your life.

Go skydiving. Purchase scuba lessons. Learn how to salsa. Go to Africa. Buy a nice dinner. Buy me a nice dinner. Whatever it is, just get off your ass. Experience.

Despite our desire to relax, people report being happiest when engaged in unique experiences.

Think back over the past month. When were you the happiest? What were you doing? When asked to a nationwide sample of over a thousand Americans, the overwhelming answer was "creating an experience."

The subjects were asked to think of two purchases over $100 that they had recently made with the purpose of increasing happiness—one a material purchase, and another an experiential purchase. Asked which purchase made them happier, the subjects were twice as likely to select the experiential purchase.

One reason experiences increase happiness more than objects do is that they're usually more novel. Positive psychologist Daniel Gilbert said,[160] "Whereas cherry floorboards generally have the same size, shape, and color on the last day of the year as they did on the first, each session of a year-long cooking class is different from the one before."

Why does that matter?

---

160 https://www.businessinsider.com/dan-gilbert-buy-experiences-not-things
-2014-10

Novelty captures our attention. An engaged mind is usually a happy mind.

Also, experiences often involve socializing, and socializing is one of the best happiness-boosting activities available to humankind.

As an example, one of my favorite experiences is the annual "nerd week" where a small group of my friends and I rent a house, play a variety of board games, and generally enjoy a great time getting away from our families.

The interesting thing (and how it relates to happiness) is we have one friend who is going through a tough financial situation. So instead of excluding him, we all chip in to cover most of his expenses for this trip.

We figure that since he's an integral part of the group, in a way, we're buying *our* happiness by making sure he can come to the nerd week each year.

In my opinion, creating a great experience (like this) is one of the best ways to spend your money.

More Information

- The Right Way to Buy Happiness[161]
- The Not-So-Secret Secret to a Happy Life[162]
- How to Buy Happiness[163]
- But Will It Make You Happy?[164]
- Spending on Experiences Instead of Possessions Results in More Satisfaction[165]
- Consuming Experience: Why Affective Forecasters Overestimate Comparative Value[166]
- To Do or to Have? That Is the Question[167]
- The Relative Relativity of Material and Experiential Purchases[168]

161   http://bucks.blogs.nytimes.com/2012/05/21/the-right-way-to-try-to-buy
-happiness/?_r=0
162   http://affordanything.com/2011/09/26/the-secret-to-happiness/
163   http://www.youtube.com/watch?v=PsihkFWDt3Y
164   http://www.nytimes.com/2010/08/08/business/08consume.html
?pagewanted=all
165   http://lifehacker.com/5608980/spend-on-experiences-instead-of
-possessions-for-longer-happiness
166   http://www.andrew.cmu.edu/user/kskassam/papers/morewedge2010.pdf
167   http://psych.colorado.edu/~vanboven/VanBoven/publications_files/vb
_gilo_2003.pdf
168   http://www.ncbi.nlm.nih.gov/pubmed/20053039

17. Practice "Active and Constructive Responding"

When people share good news, they want you to be happy with them. That's why you should develop the skill of what's commonly called "active and constructive responding," which is where you give authentic and enthusiastic responses to people when they share something important.

This habit is *especially* important when it comes to marriage and long-term relationships.

Martin Seligman said it best in his book *Flourish*:[169]

> Strangely, marriage counseling usually consists of teaching partners to fight better. This may turn an insufferable relationship into a barely tolerable one. That's not bad. **Positive psychology, however, is more interested in how to turn a good relationship into an excellent one.**

As an example, in one study,[170] 79 couples were videotaped having a discussion. Two months later, they were asked to complete a few surveys.

Those couples that used active constructive responses were significantly more likely to still be together and to report higher satisfaction with their relationship.

Seligman's book provides a good description of what active

---

169 https://www.amazon.com/Flourish-Visionary-Understanding-Happiness -Well-being/dp/1439190763

170 http://coachingtowardhappiness.com/pdf/WillYouBeThereForMeWhenT hingsGoRight.pdf

constructive responding is and isn't. Say your spouse comes home from work and says, "I received a promotion and a raise at work!"

You can respond in one of four ways:

1. Passive and Destructive: "What's for dinner?"

Nonverbal: little to no eye contact, turning away, leaving the room.

This response is uncommon. If you recognize it happening in one of your relationships, you've got a problem.

2. Active and Destructive: "That sounds like a lot of responsibility to take on. Are you going to spend even fewer nights at home now?"

Nonverbal: displays of negative emotion, such as frowning.

Don't do this, no matter how valid your concern. There is a time for reasoned discussion. First hone in on the positive. Your concerns are more likely to be recognized, and this approach will soften the impact on your relationship.

3. Passive and Constructive: "That's great! You deserve it."

This is the most common response. I see it all around me, every day. It's no surprise, as we were never taught this skill.

4. Active and Constructive: "That's great! I'm so proud of you. I know how important that promotion was to you! Where were you when your boss told you? What did he say? How did you react? We should go out and celebrate!"

Nonverbal: displays of positive emotion, touching, laughing, smiling.

Active and constructive responding is a skill that's social gold. You're taking a moment of happiness and turning it into minutes or more of enthusiastic conversation. Not only will this make both you and the other person happier, it will make it more likely that people will like you and share their positive life events with you.

Which would you rather have? Your friends sharing and talking about the positives in their life, or your friends complaining and commiserating about the negatives?

More advice from Seligman in his book:

> If you find you are not particularly good at this, plan ahead. Write down some concrete positive events that were reported to you recently. Write down how you should have responded. When you wake up in the morning, spend five minutes visualizing whom you will encounter today and what good things they are likely to tell you about themselves. Plan your active, constructive response.

Having started working on this skill, I've noticed a change in my social interactions. Many people are passionate about the good things that happen to them. If you get them started talking about those things, you'll end up with high-energy conversations.

Finally, if you'd like to learn about developing this skill (and others), I'd recommend checking out my book, *Mindful Relationship Habits: 25 Practices for Couples to Enhance Intimacy, Nurture Closeness, and Grow a Deeper Connection.*[171]

---

171   https://www.amazon.com/Mindful-Relationship-Habits-Practices -Connection-ebook/dp/B078HYGSRJ

More Information

- Active and Constructive Responding—With A Twist[172]
- Will You Be There for Me When Things Go Right?[173]

---

172   http://positivepsychologynews.com/news/doug-turner/20070515248
173   http://coachingtowardhappiness.com/pdf/WillYouBeThereForMeWhenT hingsGoRight.pdf

18. Have More Sex

Don't settle. Sex feels good. I'm sure you don't need convincing that your frequency of sex has a strong correlation with your level of happiness.

Make sex a priority.

I've been there before. You've been with the same person for a long time. The passion and lust has faded. Less frequent sex might be normal, but it's costly—less sex equals less happiness.

Check out the results from a recent study on the relationship between sex and well-being,[174]

> Respondents who reported having sex at least two to three times a month were 33 percent more likely to report a higher level of happiness than those who reported having no sex during the previous 12 months.

> The happiness effect appears to rise with frequency. Compared to those who had no sex in the previous year, those reporting a once-weekly frequency were 44 percent more likely to report a higher level of happiness, and those reporting having sex two to three times a week were 55 percent more likely.

The best advice I can give, outside of the usual, is to stop watching porn (we'll talk more about this in a later section). Evolution has not prepared your brain for today's Internet porn. The cost, *and there is a major cost to this habit,* is a reduced desire for sex. So if you have that special someone in your life, be sure

---

174   https://www.colorado.edu/today/2013/04/15/sex-happiness-hinges
-keeping-joneses-cu-boulder-study-finds

to create both the time (and the mental energy) to engage in the enjoyable activity of sex.

More Information

- Sex makes people happiest[175]
- Your Brain on Porn[176]
- A Survey Method for Characterizing Daily Life Experience: The Day Reconstruction Method[177]
- Well-Being in its Natural Habitat: Orientations to Happiness and the Experience of Everyday Activities[178]
- In sex, happiness hinges on keeping up with the Joneses, CU-Boulder study finds[179]

175   http://www.dnaindia.com/lifestyle/report-sex-makes-people-happiest-1765764

176   http://www.yourbrainonporn.com/

177   http://www.sciencemag.org/content/306/5702/1776.full

178   http://ir.canterbury.ac.nz/bitstream/10092/8040/1/thesis_fulltext.pdf

179   https://www.colorado.edu/today/2013/04/15/sex-happiness-hinges-keeping-joneses-cu-boulder-study-finds

PART 4:

FINDING HAPPINESS
BY YOURSELF

19. Laugh More

Babies are said to laugh 10 to 50 times more often than the typical adult. That's sad because laughter is powerful. The body cannot tell the difference between "fake" and "real" laughter.

If you want to be happier, you should laugh more. The fastest way to laugh more is to just laugh.

Laughter is a social tool. It exists to help us build relationships with other people. We like people who make us laugh, we like people who laugh at our jokes, and we like people who are laughing with us.

But now, let's make laughter a happiness tool.

Comedy movies and humor websites are extremely popular. Most of us actively seek out non-social laughter on a weekly basis. I often can't help but watch or read the funny things my friends share on Facebook.

Watching a 30-minute comedy show or browsing a humor website will net us, at best, a few minutes of laughter.

Be lazy.

Instead of spending an hour to get 5–10 minutes of laughter, just laugh for 5–10 minutes.

Find a place where you can be alone. If you're alone right now, that's perfect. If not, keep this in mind for the next time you are.

Okay. Just laugh. Laughing on command is a skill. Luckily, it's extremely easy to learn.

Just pretend a friend said something funny, or recall the last time you had a good laugh and replicate the experience. Yes, our bodies designed laughter to be our response to something funny. But it doesn't have to be that way—we can override our biology in this instance.

Laughter is so powerful that there is no reason not to develop this skill:

- Laughter vaporizes stress, lowering levels of cortisol and epinephrine.
- Laughter increases our pain threshold.
- Laughter improves our immunity and fights off disease.
- The mere anticipation of a good laugh immediately improves mood, reduces pain, and boosts our immune system.

It doesn't have to be loud, you can laugh *quietly* and still receive the positive benefits of this practice.

Finally, I recommend creating a trigger—an emotional state, time of day, or environmental cue after which you always laugh. As you'll learn later in this book, if you don't create a habit out of an idea, it won't help you.

So I suggest that you create a YouTube account and subscribe to the channels that make you laugh. Then whenever you need a pick-me-up, you watch a quick video and fill that moment with laughter.

More Information

- Stress Relief from Laughter? It's No Joke[180]
- The Benefits of Laughter[181]
- Laugh Your Way to Health & Happiness[182]
- Humor in Health Care: Irreverent or Invaluable?[183]
- Why Laughter May Be the Best Pain Medicine[184]
- The Laughter–Immune Connection[185]
- The Boost Before the Belly Laugh[186]

---

180   http://www.mayoclinic.com/health/stress-relief/SR00034
181   http://www.psychologytoday.com/articles/200304/the-benefits-laughter
182   http://www.sparkpeople.com/resource/wellness_articles.asp?id=655
183   https://journals.lww.com/nursing/Fulltext/2006/04000/Humor_in
_health_care__Irreverent_or_invaluable_.45.aspx
184   http://www.scientificamerican.com/article.cfm?id=why-laughter-may-be
-the-best-pain-medicine
185   http://www.hospitalclown.com/archives/vol-02/vol-2-1and2/vol2-2berk
.PDF
186   http://connection.ebscohost.com/c/articles/21455109/boost-before-belly
-laugh

20. Practice Yoga

Yoga is a special kind of exercise. A regular yoga practice increases well-being more than other types of physical activity that require the same amount of time.

One study examining strategies for countering the hedonic treadmill found[187] that the average yoga practitioner was 6% happier than the average gym buff and 15% happier than the average couch potato.

Similarly, the average person reported feeling 10% happier after leaving a yoga studio than before they entered it. Compare that to the 7% boost in happiness reported by those leaving the gym.

Why is yoga potentially more effective than exercise?

Is it the breathing in sync with your movements? The mental focus required to hold physically challenging poses? A result of exercising the entire body in slow sequence? Something to do with oxygen or CO2 levels?

Yogis will come up with all sorts of bogus explanations, mentioning imaginary concepts like chakras and oxygen infusion.

In truth, Western science is uncertain (not about chakras—they doesn't exist). One hypothesis is that yoga exercises the nervous system. Certain yoga poses and activities stimulate the fight-or-flight response while others stimulate the relaxation response. Switching back and forth between poses and activities that stimulate the parasympathetic and sympathetic nervous system

---

187   https://www.prnewswire.com/news-releases/2016-yoga-in-america-study -conducted-by-yoga-journal-and-yoga-alliance-reveals-growth-and-benefits-of -the-practice-300203418.html

potentially allows for deeper relaxation than just relaxation on its own.

Whether that hypothesis is true, yoga has nothing to do with oxygen and CO2. Our bodies are extremely good at regulating our breath and overall nervous system to optimize blood oxygen levels. Normal breathing provides arterial blood with 98–99% oxygen saturation. I've confirmed this several times in my life; even when I was stressed or breathing shallowly, the finger pulse oximeter reported back 98–99%.

The reason deep, rhythmic breathing provides benefits is that it stimulates the relaxation response and improves our heart rate variability.

Yoga is awesome. It:

- Boosts mood
- Increases flexibility
- Builds heart strength
- Tones muscles
- Encourages weight loss
- Reduces stress
- Improves pain management

There have been dozens of studies showing these benefits, so if you'd like to gain flexibility, get more exercise, and increase your happiness, you might consider building a yoga practice.

Get started by accessing the many books and videos on the subject. One of the best resources I've found is the Sarah Beth Yoga channel,[188] specifically her 10-minute yoga morning routine

---

188   https://www.youtube.com/user/SarahBethShow

for beginners video.[189] If taking up yoga seems daunting, you can begin each day with this simple routine and see if it creates a little more happiness in your life.

More Information

- Yoga—It Isn't Just for Female Hipsters[190]
- The Science of Yoga[191]
- How Yoga Makes You Happy[192]
- Getting off the hedonic treadmill, one step at a time: The impact of regular religious practice and exercise on well-being[193]
- Effect of Yogic Practices on Subjective Well Being[194]

189   https://www.youtube.com/watch?v=VaoV1PrYft4
190   http://happierhuman.com/yoga/
191   http://www.amazon.com/The-Science-Yoga-Risks-Rewards/dp
/1451641435
192   http://www.huffingtonpost.com/intent/yoga-happiness_b_2497077.html
193   http://people.duke.edu/~dandan/webfiles/PapersUpside/Religion
%20Hedonic%20Treadmill.pdf
194   http://www.ijpp.com/IJPP archives/2000_44_2/202-206.pdf

21. Do Mindfulness Meditation

Close your eyes. Focus on your breathing. When you notice your thoughts drifting, gently bring your attention back to your breath.

The "external" path to conquering the hedonic treadmill is becoming more social. The "internal" path is through meditation.

Matthieu Ricard, a Buddhist monk, is considered the happiest man alive. That title may or may not be accurate. Either way, evidence suggests that meditation rewires the brain for increased happiness.

Putting it another way, meditation is a collection of techniques developed over 2,000 years ago in order to self-generate positive emotion. The lore and philosophy involved can be ignored.

In one study,[195] participants meditated for 10 hours a week for eight weeks. Afterward, they reported a 10% decrease in anxiety, were observed to have a significant increase in left-side anterior activation in their brain (associated with positive affect), and had a stronger immune response after being given an influenza vaccine. In other words, they became less stressed, more joyful, and healthier.

There is a lot we're still learning about how meditation works—specifically, which kinds are most effective and their specific effects. For example, a meta-analysis of 813 meditation studies found that only 4% of meditation studies accounted for the placebo effect. Those 4% of studies suggested that after accounting for the placebo effect, meditation might be no more

---

195   http://www.mindingthebedside.com/wp-content/files_mf/alterationsinbr ainandimmunefunctionproducedbymindfulnessmeditation1.pdf

effective than other stress-reduction techniques, like yoga and relaxation training.

Still, anecdotal evidence suggests meditation is a worthwhile and reliable practice to boost happiness. If you'd like to practice mindfulness meditation, here is an action plan that can help you get started.

1. Define a time and a prompt for your practice.

It does not have to be the same time every day, but using a prompt such as brushing your teeth or drinking your morning tea will allow you to help get your body into the mode to meditate. It will send your brain a signal that it is time to quiet down.

2. Find a quiet place to go.

You may have a space set up in your house where you practice meditation, or you may prefer to go outside or to some other quiet place where you can feel calm. It doesn't matter where you decide to meditate, as long as it's a quiet space where you won't be interrupted.

3. Get comfortable.

Get into a physically comfortable position on a stable and solid seat. It is best to sit during meditation. However, if you feel like you might become tired or fall asleep during the practice, you may need to kneel or even stand. Loosen your clothes so nothing is holding back your breathing.

4. Pay attention to what your legs are doing.

If you are on a cushion, sit with your legs crossed comfortably in front of you. If you are sitting in a chair, gently rest the soles of your feet on the floor beneath you.

5. Sit up straight, but stay relaxed.

Allow your spine to fall into its natural, curved position. Comfort is of utmost importance here. Imagine there is a thread extending from your tailbone to the top of your head, lifting your chin and allowing you to sit up tall.

6. Think about your arms.

Loosen your arms and allow your elbows to bend slightly. Keep your upper arms parallel to your upper body, and rest your palms comfortably on your legs.

7. Soften your gaze.

Allow your chin to drop just a little, and allow your eyelids to fall slightly downward. You don't have to close your eyes—you can just allow what appears before your eyes to be there without focusing firmly on it.

8. Relax your entire body.

Scan your muscles, relaxing each one before moving to the next. Start with your toes and work your way up your entire body. Don't forget about your shoulders, face, and jaw, which are all very common areas to hold tension.

9. Think about your intention.

This doesn't have to be a long process. Begin with your basic reasons for practicing mindfulness, and your intended goals. You may be looking to feel more energized throughout the day, or you may be aiming to decrease the amount of judgment that you feel yourself thinking on a regular basis.

10. Focus on your breath.

Think about the air flowing in and out of your respiratory system as you breathe. Think about the physical sensations while you are breathing, and the rising and falling of your chest and stomach.

11. Notice when your mind begins to wander.

This is okay, and you don't want to try to force away passing thoughts. When you see your mind is wandering, gently return your focus to your breath.

12. Forgive your wandering mind.

If your mind is wandering constantly, don't fight it too much. Rather than wrestling with your thoughts, stop to observe them, and practice being able to not react. Keep sitting and paying attention. While it might be difficult to press on with your meditation, there is nothing else you can do. Keep trying to come back to your breath.

13. When you are finished, slowly lift your gaze.

There is no right or wrong amount of time to meditate, but if you are new to meditating, you may want to start with shorter sessions that last only about 10 minutes. As you become more comfortable with meditating, you can practice for longer periods of time.

14. Slowly bring your attention back to the present moment and your surroundings.

Acknowledge the space around you. Slowly begin to wiggle your fingers and toes. Next, start to move your hands and the rest of your body. Take your time getting up, and be sure to notice any sounds in your environment. Think about how your body feels in the current moment, from top to bottom. Observe your feelings and emotions.

Now if you'd like to learn more about mindfulness meditation, here are a few resources that can help you get started:

- Mindfulness Meditation—Guided 10 Minutes:[196] a video by The Honest Guys

- Headspace:[197] great guided meditations through an app

- *Search Inside Yourself:*[198] a good book on mindfulness meditation

- How to do Mindfulness Meditation:[199] a detailed walk-through of this practice

More Information

- How to Focus on Mindful Breathing Meditation[200]

- Alterations in Brain and Immune Function Produced by Mindfulness Meditation[201]

- A randomized controlled trial of mindfulness meditation versus relaxation training: Effects on distress, positive states of mind, rumination, and distraction[202]

---

196   https://www.youtube.com/watch?v=6p_yaNFSYao
197   http://www.getsomeheadspace.com/
198   http://www.amazon.com/Search-Inside-Yourself-Unexpected-Achieving/dp/0062116924
199   http://www.shambhalasun.com/index.php?id=2125&option=content&task=view
200   https://www.dummies.com/religion/spirituality/how-to-focus-on-mindful-breathing-meditation/
201   http://www.mindingthebedside.com/wp-content/files_mf/alterationsinbrainandimmunefunctionproducedbymindfulnessmeditation1.pdf
202   http://link.springer.com/article/10.1207/s15324796abm3301_2

- Meditation Practices for Health: State of the Research[203]

---

203   http://archive.ahrq.gov/downloads/pub/evidence/pdf/meditation/medit
.pdf

22. Do Loving-Kindness Meditation

Focus on someone you care about. Reflect on their positive qualities and acts of kindness they have done for you. Do whatever is most effective to generate feelings of love and compassion—visualize them at their best, repeat a mantra, or replay fond memories.

Love is happiness. But building a loving-kindness meditation practice will bring you more happiness by training your ability to generate love on a consistent basis.

A traditional Buddhist will learn and practice dozens of different kinds of meditation, but there is some evidence that loving-kindness meditation is potentially more effective in increasing well-being than mindfulness meditation. In one study,[204] just seven minutes of this type of meditation increased mood by 10–20%.

More likely, both types of meditation are complementary—both reduce stress, but together, their power is even greater. Mindfulness meditation increases emotional awareness and helps you more easily focus on the present. Loving-kindness meditation trains the ability to directly generate positive emotion, much like gratitude training.

In another study,[205] for as long as subjects meditated at least once a week, the 10–20% boost in mood persisted. Likewise, the longer they continued their practice, the more permanent the change in their baseline level of happiness became. For

204 https://www.ncbi.nlm.nih.gov/pmc/articles/PMC4468348/
205 https://www.healthline.com/nutrition/12-benefits-of-meditation

example, they could skip several practice sessions in a row without a noticeable change in their mood.

In yet another study on loving-kindness meditation,[206] "a significant correlation was found between the amount of meditation practice and innate immune and behavioral responses to psychosocial stress." In other words, the subjects became healthier and more resilient.

Loving-kindness meditation is the most empirically validated technique for enhancing compassion. It involves focusing on deliberately generating feelings of compassion, first for oneself; then for loved ones; then for friends and strangers; then, finally, for enemies.

This practice isn't hard to master. First, close your eyes and imagine someone you love and feel very warm toward. Then, instead of verbalizing a mantra, just focus on generating the emotions of compassion. Once you've got a good feel for those emotions, imagine yourself and once again try to generate feelings of compassion.

I'll admit this is one of those techniques that's hard to explain on paper, **so I recommend watching this video if you'd like to develop the habit of practicing loving-kindness meditation.**[207]

---

206   https://www.ncbi.nlm.nih.gov/pmc/articles/PMC2695992/

207   https://www.youtube.com/watch?v=sz7cpV7ERsM

More Information

- Self-Compassion—For Real Men[208]

- An Overview of Loving-kindness Meditation[209]

- Self-Compassion & Learning to Be Nicer to Ourselves[210]

- Loving-kindness meditation increases social connectedness[211]

- Open Hearts Build Lives: Positive Emotions, Induced Through Loving-Kindness Meditation, Build Consequential Personal Resources[212]

- Self-compassion and its link to adaptive psychological functioning[213]

- Effect of compassion meditation on neuroendocrine, innate immune and behavioral responses to psychosocial stress[214]

- The Science of Compassion[215]

---

208   http://happierhuman.com/self-compassion/
209   http://www.buddhanet.net/metta_in.htm
210   http://tinybuddha.com/blog/self-compassion-learning-to-be-nicer-to-ourselves/
211   https://www.ncbi.nlm.nih.gov/pubmed/18837623
212   http://www.ncbi.nlm.nih.gov/pmc/articles/PMC3156028/
213   http://self-compassion.org/wp-content/uploads/publications/JRP.pdf
214   http://www.ncbi.nlm.nih.gov/pmc/articles/PMC2695992/
215   http://happierhuman.com/the-science-of-compassion/

23. Reminisce

Take photos. Make an album. Collect souvenirs. Take a few moments to relive a positive experience, using photos or souvenirs to jog your memory.

The happiness that comes from reminiscing is as real as the happiness that comes from the actual experience.

As someone firmly focused on the future, I never used to take time to reminisce. That was a mistake; I was missing out on an opportunity to create happiness as well as an opportunity to develop my sense of self.

However, when you take the time to look back on your memories, experiences, and great interactions, you can inject a little bit of happiness into your day.

In his book *The Time Paradox*,[216] Philip Zimbardo makes the claim that those who frequently reminisce about positive life events are the most likely to be happy. Further, he found that the average American spends very little time reminiscing compared to other nationalities. Perhaps that is one reason we don't rank in top 10 happiest countries, despite having the most wealth and power.

Now, this is a straightforward concept. If you'd like to reminisce on a regular basis, here are a few strategies to get started:

- Always carry a camera (or cell phone) with you and take pictures of everyday events. Then put your photos in

---

216   https://www.amazon.com/The-Time-Paradox-Psychology-Change/dp/B002BWQ4Q4

easy-to-find categories that allow you to revisit snippets of your life.

- Make a scrapbook of your past mementos.
- Call an old friend.
- Write a gratitude letter to people who have made a difference in your life.
- Watch old movies that you love.
- Listen to music you enjoyed when you were younger.
- Start a diary and chronicle important parts of your life.

Bottom line: If you build a habit where you're frequently capturing the little moments in your life, you'll have a collection of memories you can access whenever you feel the need to remember the good times.

More Information

- A List of Reminiscing Activities[217]
- *The Time Paradox*[218]
- Time Perspective and Correlates of Wellbeing[219]
- Happiness and reminiscing: The role of time perspective, affect, and mode of thinking[220]

217   https://caregiversactivitysource.com/activities-for-elderly/reminiscing-activities-for-the-elderly/
218   http://www.amazon.com/The-Time-Paradox-Psychology-Change/dp/B002BWQ4Q4
219   http://tas.sagepub.com/content/17/1/47.short
220   http://psycnet.apa.org/journals/psp/49/6/1460/

24. Create Anticipation

Do you remember that feeling of the night before Christmas (or your favorite holiday), of being so excited and full of anticipation that you couldn't fall asleep?

Or even more recently, imagine that next Friday you're doing something you've been looking forward to: hanging out with good friends, going to a sporting event, meeting me in person, whatever.

What's interesting is not only are you happy on the day of the event, you're feeling levels of excitement in the days *leading up* to the event.

That's because the happiness that comes from anticipation is as real as the happiness that comes from actual experiences.

You can apply this strategy in many small ways throughout your life: Pay now and consume later. Take a few moments to review upcoming events you're looking forward to. Instead of reading the book all at once, read only one chapter at a time. Instead of playing that new game for 10 hours straight, stop after an hour. Savor, anticipate, and then play some more.

The happiness a positive event brings us is proportional to the amount of time we spend thinking about it. Being given an awesome gift will bring no happiness if we are too preoccupied worrying about work.

More happiness can be produced by that gift by anticipating the gift, savoring, and focusing our attention on the gift when we receive it, *and* reminiscing on the gift afterward.

There is a part of our brain like a raging bull that doesn't care about our happiness and wants us to move forward as fast as possible. Tame that beast.

Anticipating is not the same thing as fantasizing. Fantasizing involves raising expectations—producing pleasure now at the expense of happiness during the actual experience. Anticipation involves being happy that a future event is about to occur, as it will actually occur, not as some idealized fantasy.

Research suggests that an organic method of increasing anticipation is to (1) have a large social network (which results in being invited to more events and social interactions that you can anticipate), and (2) have a high number of steps in place to achieve your goals (which results in more progress). However, there is one strategy you can implement immediately. Pay now and consume later.

It's tough, and I often fail, but when I succeed, it's always worth it. Not only do I get lots of happiness from the anticipation, I find that withholding something from myself, even after I've purchased it, has the effect of increasing my level of savoring when I do get around to consuming it. Examples from my own life include episodes of my favorite TV show, books, video games, and sweets.

Jeroen Nawijn, lead author of a study of vacation-goers,[221] says, "The practical lesson for an individual is that you derive most of your happiness from anticipating the holiday trip."

---

221   https://well.blogs.nytimes.com/2010/02/18/how-vacations-affect-your -happiness/

There are three simple techniques you can use to add more anticipation to your life:

1. Buy many small pleasures.

Splitting up large purchases into small ones can increase total pleasure by sidestepping the curse of adaptation. This applies as much to the moment of consumption as to the anticipation of consumption.

Each additional serving (cookie, drink, TV show, video game, pair of jeans, etc.) produces less pleasure *and less anticipation* than the last one.

In a world without adaptation, the anticipation of eating 10 cookies at once would be 10 times greater than the anticipation of eating just one. In our world, 10 cookies at once provides only two to five times as much anticipatory pleasure as one cookie.

You can easily confirm this for yourself.

Imagine that at the end of this week you'll be presented with one serving of your favorite dessert. Feel the anticipation. Now imagine that you'll be presented with 10 servings of your favorite dessert, which you must eat at once.

Did you experience 10X as much anticipation?

Odds are, you didn't.

The second option has got a lot more anticipation action going for it.

Although each individual event provides less anticipatory pleasure, the combined total pleasure is much larger.

The actual numbers are arbitrary, but the underlying principal is not. **Building small pleasures into your life increases your overall enjoyment.**

2. Pay now and consume later.

How much would you be willing to pay to kiss your favorite celebrity three hours from now? How about three days from now?

In a study asking exactly that question,[222] people were willing to pay 37% more for the second option than for the first. There were other options too. As long as the wait wasn't too long, like 10 years, people were willing to pay more.

The extra hours, days, and weeks gave people more time to anticipate their sweet and sexy hypothetical kiss.

The strategy is easy to understand: **purchase now and consume later.** It's not as easy to implement.

Lucky for us, this is a two for in one—get more pleasure from your money *and* develop your self-control skills.

The first two are self-explanatory. By consuming later, we increase anticipatory pleasure while exercising our self-control muscle.

The third is a bonus; more anticipation also equals more pleasure during consumption.

3. Create anticipation triggers.

Tie together a trigger with the mental action of anticipation. That is what I call happiness magic: just by taking a moment to anticipate, you're creating happiness out of nothing.

---

222   https://www.happierhuman.com/money-and-happiness-2/

You can do this throughout the day. Like, when you:

- Are hungry, *anticipate* the next meal you will be eating
- Take a shower, *anticipate* your weekend plans
- Are bored, *anticipate* the next fun thing you will be doing
- Are tired, *anticipate* your next workout
- See your loved one, *anticipate* your next night out
- Finish watching a show you like, *anticipate* the next episode
- Finish reading a chapter of a book you like, *anticipate* the next chapter

So what about you?

Ask yourself:

How can I bring more anticipatory happiness into my life?

25. Think Counterfactually

Think about something that brings you great happiness—your child, your health, your job, whatever. Now, either think of ways in which it's surprising that you actually have this thing, or spend time visualizing an alternate world where this thing doesn't exist or has been taken from you.

Simply put:

We most appreciate something after we've lost it. Luckily, you can pretend to lose something in order to increase your appreciation (and happiness) for it.

For example, in which circumstance do you think a father will better appreciate his daughter—the norm, during which he awakens and takes her continued existence for granted, or after a nightmare in which she was run over by a truck?

The question is: Is the happiness created by the better appreciation greater than the unhappiness created by imagining her death?

In the case of a nightmare, I can't say. **But in studies of counterfactual thinking, temporarily imagining loss has the long-term effect of increasing happiness.**

The primary technique used by the Stoics to cultivate tranquility and happiness was exactly as I described above. By temporarily imagining deep loss, the rest of the day was spent with greater appreciation and joy.

In one study,[223] couples were asked either to describe ways in

---

223   https://www.ncbi.nlm.nih.gov/pmc/articles/PMC2746912/

which their being together was expected, or ways in which it was unexpected. Although couples expected to increase their relationship satisfaction and temporarily boost their mood by describing ways in which their relationship was destined, the results came out the opposite.

Those who followed the instructions below saw a 10 to 20% increase in their relationship satisfaction and mood:

"Please describe ways that this thing or event might never have happened or might never have been part of your life," and "Please describe ways in which it is SURPRISING that this thing or event is part of your life."

This is why those who experience deep suffering often rebound and experience great gratitude and happiness afterward. When you realize you might not have had your amazing romantic partner—that it was only by crazy coincidence you were both at the right place at the right time—gratitude (and therefore satisfaction and happiness), goes way up.

Now, if you'd like to develop the practice of counterfactual thinking, I'd like to point you to the simple process outlined in Danni Peck's article, "Everything You Need to Know about Counterfactual Thinking."[224]

First, when reviewing the details of a major life event, think of the other possible scenarios that could have happened. It makes you feel that the one final outcome was fated/destined to happen.

If you have a negative experience, imagine two desirable but completely different and positive outcomes. This way, you train

---

224 https://www.betterhelp.com/advice/general/everything-you-need-to -know-about-counterfactual-thinking/

your mind to avoid falling into and dwelling on self-pitying thoughts.

After you've imaged the positive outcomes, think now of other series of actions that would still generate the negative experience you're having. This "even-if" thinking helps you pinpoint the things that led to the negative experience to help you avoid the same pitfall in the future.

Third, envision that you go through all the actions that led to the negative experience. Only this time, the outcome is favorable. This helps you gain the perspective that there are so many things in life that happen beyond your control.

Finally, think of a resulting experience that is more negative or undesirable than the one you currently have. Since many things can be beyond our control, thinking counterfactually can give us a very positive feeling of closure.

More Information

- How to Be Grateful When You Don't Feel Like It[225]
- Negative Visualization and Gratitude[226]
- A Guide to the Good Life: The Ancient Art of Stoic Joy[227]
- It's a Wonderful Life: Mentally Subtracting Positive Events Improves People's Affective States, Contrary to Their Affective Forecasts[228]

---

225 http://www.raptitude.com/2009/05/how-to-be-grateful-when-you-dont-feel-like-it/

226 http://axoplasm.com/blog/negative-visualization-and-gratitude/

227 http://www.amazon.com/Guide-Good-Life-Ancient-Stoic/dp/0195374614

228 http://www.ncbi.nlm.nih.gov/pmc/articles/PMC2746912/

- From What Might Have Been to What Must Have Been: Counterfactual Thinking Creates Meaning[229]

---

[229] http://www.haas.berkeley.edu/groups/online_marketing/facultyCV /papers/kray_paper2010.pdf

26. Maybe Think Fast

I'll admit that this next idea is a little "out there," but hear me out.

Drink some caffeine, turn on some fast music, and put on your game face. Speed up. Read twice as fast as you normally would, get your work done as quickly as possible, brainstorm more ideas than you normally would; whatever it takes, think fast.

Being happy speeds up your brain. But the relationship also works in reverse—speeding up your brain will make you happier.

Those moments when we're tired, we usually feel the worst. Likewise, those moments when energy is abundant, desire is high, and work seems effortless are when we usually feel the best. Energy is happiness. This is why cold showers, exercise, caffeine, and excitement usually make us happy; they give us energy.

A series of six experiments[230] showed that each of four different ways of inducing fast thought, either by making participants read fast, make quick decisions, brainstorm quickly, or watch TV that had been sped up, caused participants to feel happier.

It's unclear why artificially thinking fast causes an increase in mood. It could be because thinking fast causes the release of dopamine, because we enjoy thinking fast, or because thinking fast tricks a part of our brain into thinking we've got lots of energy, which in turn causes happiness.

It's difficult to sustain artificial fast thinking. However, there is

---

230   https://dash.harvard.edu/bitstream/handle/1/2381051/pronin
_psychologicaleffects.pdf?sequence=4

some good news. First, many forms of inducing fast thinking cause changes that can last for several hours, like exercise, drinking caffeine, and listening to fast music. Second, fast thinking can trigger increased mood, which in turn can trigger fast thinking. In other words, fast thinking can trigger a positive cycle.

Indeed, that is the case for most of the hacks on this page—being happy increases the likelihood of engaging in actions that will cause future happiness, like working harder or being friendlier.

Now, if you'd like to learn to speed up your thoughts, here are a few ideas to help you get started:

- **Have your eyes and ears checked.** It's worth the trip to the doctor. We receive most of the information from our environment through our eyes and ears. Defects in your eyesight or hearing can impair the way you process information.

- **Think and work on your feet.** A recent study[231] revealed that comprehension and time-management skills, as well as memory, are enhanced or improved when people work at standing desks.

- **Speed-read by focusing on reading comprehension.** The technique is proven to increase your brain's ability to read faster.

- **Get enough sleep.** Getting the right amount of sleep is one of the most essential things you can do to keep your brain functioning at an optimal level.

- **Engage your brain in a "brain training program."** There are

---

231   http://www.ntxe-news.com/cgi-bin/artman/exec/view.cgi?archive=71& num=101198

science-backed programs that provide training to develop and speed up your thought-processing abilities.

- **Keep temperature at an optimal level.** There is a correlation between temperature and the speed of our thought processes. The optimal temperature for faster cognition is around 72 degrees.

- **Meditate regularly.** Regular meditation encourages the formation and healing of neural pathways and brain cells, and it increases the plasticity of the brain. Meditating can help speed up your mental processing—your ability to concentrate and your capacity to learn new things.

- **As much as possible, avoid foods and medications that slow down your thinking processes.** Certain foods and excessive amounts of sugar can disrupt the communication between brain cells, thus slowing your thoughts. Certain medications can impair your cognitive functions. It's highly recommended that you ask your doctor about the side effects of your prescription.

- **Exercise.** Exercise improves focus, concentration, and fact retention.

- **Play a musical instrument.** Studies have shown that playing a musical instrument[232] improves cognitive functions.

- **Read a book.** Reading a good piece of literature can improve cognitive functions and enhance your ability for imagination.

What's great about these suggestions is many of them not only help you think faster, they are also other strategies to increase happiness we have mentioned in this book (i.e., meditation,

---

232 https://www.inc.com/john-rampton/the-benefits-of-playing-music-help -your-brain-more.html

exercising, and getting a full night's rest.) So if you're unsure of where to start, I'd suggest picking one of those three habits.

More Information

- Rapid Thinking Makes People Happy[233]
- Smile! It Could Make You Happier[234]
- Thought Speed, Mood, and the Experience of Mental Motion[235]
- The Effect of Mental Progression on Mood[236]
- Psychological effects of thought acceleration[237]
- Manic thinking: Independent effects of thought speed and thought content on mood[238]

---

233 http://www.scientificamerican.com/article.cfm?id=rapid-thinking-makes -people-happy

234 http://www.scientificamerican.com/article.cfm?id=smile-it-could-make -you-happier

235 https://pdfs.semanticscholar.org/d117/fcfe1d0d20f2a4503b5725759c19a 82aadfb.pdf

236 https://www.ncbi.nlm.nih.gov/pubmed/21823806

237 https://dash.harvard.edu/bitstream/handle/1/2381051/pronin _psychologicaleffects.pdf?sequence=4

238 http://www.ncbi.nlm.nih.gov/pubmed/16984299

27. Reflect on Your Strengths and Victories

Instead of stressing out or ruminating on a recent embarrassment or failure, reflect on your strengths or a past victory.

The truth is, we tend to take things for granted. Not just others and their contributions, but also our own strengths.

If you find yourself lacking confidence and doubting your ability, instead of focusing on the negatives, as the mind is likely to do, focus on your positives—your persistence, social skills, intelligence, or one of other possible strengths[239] that many people have.

No two humans are the same. Some have more strengths than others. But by taking the time to read this book, you've already demonstrated several strengths that many humans don't have, like open-mindedness, curiosity, hope, and desire for change.

If you're not sure of your strengths, ask others to describe a time when you've been at your best, or take a test that helps you better understand your unique advantages. Here are three useful websites to help you get started:

- The CliftonStrengths Test[240]
- Reflected Best Self Exercise™[241]
- Character Strength's Test[242]

Now, if you *do* know what your strengths are but still lack

---

239   http://www.meaningandhappiness.com/psychology-research/list-of
-personal-strengths.html
240   https://www.gallupstrengthscenter.com/Purchase/
241   https://positiveorgs.bus.umich.edu/cpo-tools/rbse/
242   https://www.viacharacter.org/survey

confidence, when you notice your thoughts drifting to how you're incapable, try to redirect them to the two cores of your foundation—times when you've overcome challenges, and the areas of your life where you possess strengths many others don't.

Reflecting on how you're incapable is likely to sap your energy and make you unhappy. Reflecting on how you're capable is likely to energize you and make you happy. It's not good to be overconfident and disconnected from reality, but underestimating your strengths makes you as disconnected as overestimating them.

Most humans are capable of more than they think. Likewise, most humans have already overcome many challenges. Living inside of our own brains, stuck watching life through the same pair of eyes, we fail to recognize that what is exciting or easy for us is often challenging for many others.

Research shows that those who are aware of and focus on their strengths are happier than those who aren't and don't.

More Information

- Elevate your talents with the CliftonStrengths[243]
- List of Personal Strengths[244]
- Reflected Best Self Exercise™[245]
- The Power of Affirming Your Values
- Benefits of Self-Affirmation[246]

---

243   https://www.gallupstrengthscenter.com/Purchase/
244   http://www.meaningandhappiness.com/psychology-research/list-of
-personal-strengths.html
245   https://positiveorgs.bus.umich.edu/cpo-tools/rbse/
246   http://www.cmu.edu/homepage/health/2013/summer/benefits-of-self
-affirmation.shtml

- Self-Control Instantly Replenished by Self-Affirmation[247]
- Composing the Reflected Best-Self Portrait: Building Pathways for Becoming Extraordinary in Work Organizations[248]

---

247 http://www.spring.org.uk/2010/03/self-control-instantly-replenished-by
-self-affirmation.php

248 http://webuser.bus.umich.edu/janedut/pos/best self from amr.pdf

28. Maybe Consume Caffeine

Here's another idea that's a *little* controversial, which is why I consider this to be a "maybe" idea for increasing happiness. So feel free to read on *or* skip to the next habit.

In some studies, it was found that adding a small amount of caffeine to your diet can increase your overall happiness.

Caffeine gives us energy, is used by those with depression as over-the-counter medication, and boosts mood.

In other words, **caffeine in moderation is more effective than caffeine consumed throughout the day.**

People respond differently to caffeine. For that reason, many who consume caffeine in moderation experience net total benefits. But the research suggests most heavy consumers are getting little benefit or even a negative benefit.

How can caffeine be negative?

One word: **Tolerance.**

Caffeine increases mood and energy level. In order to maintain homeostasis, the body will counter those effects by reducing mood and reducing levels of energy. In this way, although a foreign, potentially harmful substance is entering the body and influencing the brain, the body can maintain control over the situation.

In this case, it would be better if the brain didn't maintain balance—zero tolerance and easy energy would be great. But it does. Studies find that among those who consume large quantities of caffeine, like two venti coffees a day, their tolerance and adaptation to coffee consumption is so large that, on average, their baseline level of happiness has decreased.

On the other hand, for those who consume in moderation—say two sodas a day or one coffee in the morning—there is tolerance and adaptation, but net, their level of happiness will be on average higher than if they weren't consuming.

So if caffeine is an important part of your routine, here are two basic rules to make sure you're maximizing the results (for your happiness) without experiencing many of its downsides:

First, pace out your consumption by six to eight hours.

More frequent consumption builds tolerance and can lead to withdrawal symptoms, which can worsen your mood and energy levels and create anxiety. In one study of coffee consumption,[249] those who drank coffee in the morning and then again two more times, four hours apart, actually felt worse than the control group. Those who drank coffee just twice, once in the morning and once eight hours later, had the best results.

Second, don't drink coffee four to six hours before you sleep.

You may think it's not impacting your sleep. Let's get real—it is. You may still find it easy to go to sleep, but the quality and depth your sleep is suffering.

Sleep quality[250] is one of the most important contributors to mood. Not only can caffeine mask sleep issues by providing artificial stimulation, but caffeine can also perpetuate a cycle of degrading your sleep, which in turn makes you more tired and

---

249   https://www.spring.org.uk/2013/08/what-caffeine-really-does-to-your
-brain.php

250   http://counsellingresource.com/features/2006/05/06/sleep-mood/

requires you to consume even more caffeine. It may be incredibly hard to cut back to twice a day and to avoid caffeine at night, but it's worth the effort.

If you do the math with these two rules, you'll see you shouldn't consume more than three or four servings of caffeine per day. That's enough to elevate your mood without causing too much of an addiction.

More Information

- What Caffeine Really Does to Your Brain[251]

- Cognitive and psychomotor performance, mood, and pressor effects of caffeine after 4, 6 and 8 h caffeine abstinence[252]

- Cognitive and mood improvements of caffeine in habitual consumers and habitual non-consumers of caffeine[253]

- Caffeine withdrawal, acute effects, tolerance, and absence of net beneficial effects of chronic administration: cerebral blood flow velocity, quantitative EEG, and subjective effects[254]

- Central and peripheral effects of sustained caffeine use: tolerance is incomplete[255]

- A comparison of the effects of caffeine following abstinence and normal caffeine use[256]

251 http://www.spring.org.uk/2013/08/what-caffeine-really-does-to-your-brain.php

252 http://www.ncbi.nlm.nih.gov/pubmed/15696321

253 https://www.ncbi.nlm.nih.gov/pubmed/15678363

254 http://www.ncbi.nlm.nih.gov/pubmed/19241060

255 http://www.ncbi.nlm.nih.gov/pubmed/12392588

256 http://www.ncbi.nlm.nih.gov/pubmed/19777214

- Psychological effects of dietary components of tea: caffeine and L-theanine[257]

257   http://www.ncbi.nlm.nih.gov/pubmed/18254874

29. Live Close to Work

Thinking of purchasing a new house? Choose a place close to work, even if the place is smaller or in a poorer neighborhood.

Annie Lowrey[258] says it best:

> Couples in which one partner commutes for longer than 45 minutes are 40 percent likelier to divorce.

The location of your house is a trade-off, but not the kind you're thinking.

Because of the hedonic treadmill, many of the benefits you expect your new home to give you will quickly fizzle out. Assuming you don't live in a closet under the stairs like Harry Potter, the size of your home only has a *small impact* on your overall happiness.

Why?

Because over time, the increased size becomes less novel, and you start to take it for granted.

The same is true if you're choosing a longer commute in order to save money. Except for those living below the poverty line, disposable income has a smaller impact on life satisfaction than commute time.

Happiness is not about accumulating accomplishments and material objects—happiness is about the quality of your day-to-day experience.

---

258   https://slate.com/business/2011/05/long-commutes-cause-obesity-neck -pain-loneliness-divorce-stress-and-insomnia.html

This means that a frustrating commute adds frustration to your life ...

Every. Single. Workday!

Furthermore, a higher disposable income is unlikely to have an offsetting positive impact every single day. We quickly adapt to most of the goodies we purchase. But do we adapt to a frustrating commute? Most of the time the answer is no.

In one study,[259] 1,018 employed Americans were randomly pinged throughout the day, asking how they were feeling and what they were doing. The subjects consistently reported feeling the worst at two times of the day: during their commute to and from work. The subjects reported feeling happier even when working and doing housework.

If you care about your well-being and the well-being of your family, take the data seriously; a long commute truly does increase your risk of divorce. All that frustration is poisonous. You think you'll manage, but after a few weeks or months, your patience will wear thin.

So if you want to instantly feel better on a daily basis, take a hard look at the average time it takes to commute and how you can change it for the better.

---

259   https://link.springer.com/article/10.1007/s11205-012-0003-2

More Information

- Your Commute Is Killing You[260]
- Commuting[261]
- Stress that Doesn't Pay: The Commuting Paradox[262]
- A Survey Method for Characterizing Daily Life Experience: The Day Reconstruction Method[263]
- Happiness and Satisfaction with Work Commute[264]

---

260 http://www.slate.com/articles/business/moneybox/2011/05/your
_commute_is_killing_you.html

261 http://scienceblogs.com/cortex/2010/03/30/commuting/

262 https://onlinelibrary.wiley.com/doi/abs/10.1111/j.1467-9442.2008.00542
.x

263 http://www.sciencemag.org/content/306/5702/1776.full

264 http://link.springer.com/article/10.1007/s11205-012-0003-2/fulltext
.html

30. Buy Many Small Things

Instead of purchasing an expensive computer, remodeling your house, or buying a fast car, purchase many small things—a dozen romantic evenings out with your loved one, a weekly indulgence of fancy chocolate or massage, some nice candles, or some music for your iPhone.

In the words of Elizabeth Dunn:[265]

> If we inevitably adapt to the greatest delights that money can buy, than [sic] it may be better to indulge in a variety of frequent, small pleasures.

Imagine that you're hungry, about to eat some pizza. The first slice will taste delicious. Perhaps you've got a large appetite and will also enjoy slices two and three. But slices four and five? They'll give you more stomach ache than pleasure. You're adapting. Money works in a similar way.

Fulfill a basic need → happiness.

So you need to get around town? Buy a car → happiness.

Let's say you trade in the car and decide to splurge, purchasing something twice as expensive.

Will you get twice as much happiness?

No.

Once the basic need is met, everything on top has a diminishing impact. The luxury interior and smoother acceleration are nice but are not as valuable as the base ability to drive.

---

265   https://scholar.harvard.edu/files/danielgilbert/files/if-money-doesnt-make-you-happy.nov-12-20101.pdf

The extra money spent upgrading to a luxury car could have been spent purchasing a dozen weekend getaways. The research suggests those dozen getaways would produce at least twice as much happiness as the luxury car.

Here are a few examples from the research. Folks reported a greater total increase in happiness from:

- Experiencing two positive events at different times, rather than both at once
- Eating two 6-ounce cookies at different times, rather than one 12-ounce cookie at once
- Imagining themselves winning a $25 lottery then a $50 lottery, rather than winning a $75 lottery all at once
- Listening to a song they enjoyed with a pause in the middle, rather than all at once

Folks with more frequent positive emotions are more likely to report being happy than those with less frequent but more intense positive emotions. That's good because creating small mood bumps throughout the day is easier and much cheaper than creating one or two intense thrills.

The lesson here? Look for small purchases that inject a little bit of happiness throughout your day.

More Information

- Money Secret #1: Buy Many Small Pleasures[266]
- Why You Should Embrace the Small Pleasures[267]
- Why Many Small Pleasures Beat Fewer Larger Ones[268]
- Happiness is the Frequency, Not the Intensity, of Positive Versus Negative Affect[269]
- Preferences for separating or combining events[270]
- Objective Happiness[271]
- Mental Accounting and Consumer Choice[272]

266   http://happierhuman.com/money-and-happiness-1/
267   http://www.forbes.com/sites/dorieclark/2012/02/29/why-you-should
-embrace-the-small-pleasures/
268   http://www.spring.org.uk/2011/10/why-many-small-pleasures-beat
-fewer-larger-ones.php
269   http://link.springer.com/chapter/10.1007/978-90-481-2354-4_10
270   http://www.ncbi.nlm.nih.gov/pubmed/1995835
271   http://profron.net/happiness/files/readings/Kahneman
_ObjectiveHappiness.pdf
272   http://wolfweb.unr.edu/homepage/pingle/Teaching/BADM 791/Week 9
Behavioral Microeconomics/Thaler-Mental Accountingr.pdf

31. Enjoy a Hobby

Do you have a hobby or activity that relaxes you?

Many people find themselves stuck in a daily or weekly routine that offers little more than a "rinse and repeat" lifestyle. But what happens when that routine becomes dull and overly predictable. One thing you can do is focus on a hobby that not only breaks up the monotony, but also injects a dose of happiness into your daily existence.

Spending time doing an enjoyable activity that is not attached to work or other commitments will help increase your happiness and satisfaction with life. It will allow you to spend time doing something that is only for your own personal benefit and not the benefit of others.

With the right hobby, you will create a multitude of mental and health benefits.

For instance, hobbies:

- **Are a great stress reliever:** They should be completely pleasurable activities that take your mind off the demands of your daily life or negative emotions. It's a great outlet for releasing stress.

- **Encourage you to take a break:** They offer you an opportunity to take a break while giving you a sense of purpose.

- **Help transition you to retirement:** While the idea of retirement may seem like a great thing, many people find that their lives lose purpose once they stop working. Having a hobby will give you a life outside of work, so you can have something productive to focus on. Many people learn to play bridge in their later years in order to keep an active social life while also challenging their minds.

- **Allow you to explore yourself and your talents:** You never know what you're capable of unless you try something. Hobbies can make you do that.

- **Help you grow spiritually:** When you've pushed yourself to the limit to achieve something, you tend to feel good about yourself. This can be an internal motivation to continue to grow.

- **Help ward off depression.** Studies have shown that habits can decrease feelings of anxiety. Hobbies help improve a person's sense of identity, usefulness, and well-being, and eliminate feelings of worthlessness and self-doubt.

- **Allow you to meet new people:** Hobbies offer a way of connecting with people who have similar interests. Hanging out with like-minded people who share your passions can be an effective way to increase your social circle.

- **Enable you to give back:** Giving back is a win-win. It helps others and creates in you a feeling of usefulness and a sense of purpose, removing the feelings of worthlessness and self-doubt.

- **Make you more interesting:** You may gain a different perspective on things than other people. Hobbies can also help you learn something about other cultures in some instances.

- **Help you become more patient:** When you're learning something new, things don't usually go right the first try. When you are patient enough to go through the baby steps in order to master a hobby, achieving success for the first time (e.g., in fishing) will feel so rewarding and fulfilling.

- **Can help improve your career:** Having a hobby helps you learn how to handle work-life stress and think creatively. A hobby can also help decrease your chances of burnout at work.

So if you're stuck figuring out how to best use your free time, I suggest blocking out time where you can focus on a hobby that makes you happy.

32. Maybe Get a Standing Desk

There's been a lot of hype recently surrounding the standing desk. But here's the reality: more than 95% of the folks who get a standing desk stop using it after a few weeks.

Using a standing desk *will* make you happier. The first few days will be like hell—your legs will hurt and then hurt some more. But as long as you stand in moderation, say use your standing desk half the day and sit during the rest, you'll be okay.

Still not convinced about the value of increasing how long you stand each day? Well, here are a number of health benefits you'll receive if you commit to this habit:

- Standing reduces the risk of weight gain and obesity. Men and women who stand for up to six hours per day have 59% and 35% reduced likelihood of becoming obese, respectively.

- Compared with sitting, standing lowers the risk of heart disease. Substituting at least a couple hours a day can lower bad cholesterol levels by up to 11%.

- Standing can help ease or reduce chronic back pain. A study on back pain done by Stanford University[273] reveals that people who use sit-stand desks instead of regular desks while at work were more likely to report pain-free days.

- Standing helps reduce the risk of cancer. Quite a number of cases of breast and colon cancers are caused by inactivity, making prolonged sitting one of the largest cancer risks.

---

273 http://journals.lww.com/joem/Citation/2016/03000/Impact_of_a_Sit
_Stand_Workstation_on_Chronic_Low.11.aspx

Engaging in short bouts of activity, such as standing and walking, can help protect against many cancers.

- Standing helps decrease the risk of type 2 diabetes and other metabolic diseases. Breaking up your time of prolonged sitting by standing up on a regular basis can reduce blood sugar levels by 34%.

- Standing while working boosts productivity. In one study,[274] call center agents who used a stand-capable desk for over six months were found to be more productive than those who used regular desks.

- Standing helps increase energy levels and improve mood. Standing while working improves collaboration and encourages creativity.[275] Workers who use standing desks report less stress and fatigue[276] than those who don't.

- Standing while working helps tone muscles. It also helps improve your posture and balance.

So not only will standing increase your happiness, but it'll also have a positive spillover effect into many other areas of your life.

On a personal, anecdotal level, I know a dozen or so people who have tried implementing the standing desk. At first, it will be a very *hard* habit to develop. That's why most people don't stick it out.

So if you're interested in implementing this concept, I suggest you don't invest a lot of money *until* you know for certain that you'll stick to this habit. That's why I recommend this Lifehack

274   http://www.tandfonline.com/doi/abs/10.1080/21577323.2016.1183534
275   http://journals.sagepub.com/doi/abs/10.1177/1948550614538463
276   https://www.ncbi.nlm.nih.gov/pubmed/23057991

article,[277] which profiles a variety of inexpensive standing desk options.

On the other hand, since this is a challenging habit, you might find it easier to implement some of the other ideas covered in this book first (especially the first nine strategies that we've already covered). Once you've mastered the easier habits, you can come back to this idea and incorporate a standing desk into your daily routine.

More Information

- The Hidden Psychological Benefits of a Standing Desk[278]
- What Are The Advantages and Disadvantages of Standing Desks?[279]

---

277   https://www.lifehack.org/579631/high-quality-and-cheap-standing-desk -for-2017

278   http://lifehacker.com/the-hidden-psychological-benefits-of-a-standing -desk-955696631

279   http://www.forbes.com/sites/quora/2012/07/16/what-are-the-advantages -and-disadvantages-of-standing-desks/

33. Sit Up Straight

Confident people with lots of self-esteem puff out their chests. The relationship isn't one-way. Puffing out your chest and sitting up straight can increase your self-esteem and levels of energy.

Slouching doesn't just make you look bad—it can make you feel bad too!

One study[280] done at Ohio State University and published in the *Journal of Behavior Therapy and Experimental Psychiatry* showed that people who adopt upright postures while sitting tend to feel less anxious and have lower negative emotions than people who sit with their regular or slumped postures.

Another study done by a group from the University of Auckland[281] revealed that sitting upright helps a person cope better with stress. Sitting up straight in the face of stressful events decreases a person's tendency to be in a negative mood, and it helps maintains self-esteem.

The following tips can help you develop the habit of sitting up straight for better posture and happiness:

- Ideally, if you're working on a computer, the screen should be a little below eye level.

- When your work keeps you at a desk, make sure that both your feet are planted on the floor and your knees are bent at a right angle and aligned with the hips.

- Take a break by standing up, walking, or stretching every 20 minutes. Avoid being in a sitting position for prolonged

---

280   https://www.sciencedirect.com/science/article/pii/S0005791616301719
281   https://www.ncbi.nlm.nih.gov/pubmed/25222091

periods of time (more than half an hour), as you put more strain on your spine and pelvis with prolonged sitting.

- Make sure you're not putting your body in awkward positions whenever you're sitting down. Keep shoulders back, evenly distribute your weight on your hips, and keep your back straight.

- When you're sitting, release any tension you feel in your jaws, shoulders, and hips.

- To have better muscular support while you're sitting, it's a good idea to also do core-strengthening and stretching exercises. Try trunk rotation, abdominal presses (single-leg), and bridge. These exercises strengthen your upper back and core.

So if you'd like to be happier on a more consistent basis, pay attention to your posture and how it's affecting your mood.

More Information

- The Science of Posture: Sitting up straight will make you happier, more confident and less risk-averse[282]

- Your Body Language May Shape Who You Are[283]

- Body Posture Effects on Self-evaluation: A Self-validation Approach[284]

---

282 http://blog.bufferapp.com/improve-posture-good-posture-science -happiness

283 http://www.youtube.com/watch?v=Ks-_Mh1QhMc

284 http://onlinelibrary.wiley.com/doi/10.1002/ejsp.607/abstract

34. Maybe Take Omega-3 Supplements

Some recent evidence suggests that omega-3 fatty acid consumption can *slightly* improve mental health and happiness.

That said, there is conflicting information on this nutrient and how it relates to happiness, so this is another idea that's in the "maybe" category.

As an example, several large studies have found that those who consume less fish, that is those who get less omega-3, are more likely to develop depression.

On the other hand, a recent meta-analysis of almost 100 omega-3 studies found that having subjects increase their intake of omega-3 did nothing to increase their levels of happiness or reduce their risk of developing depression.

What's going on? Why do some studies show that omega-3 increases happiness, while others show no effect?

There is a scientific phenomenon called *publication bias*. Let's say in one study, a research lab gives some people omega-3 supplements. Two months later, those people report being happier. That's interesting. Therefore, that study is likely to get accepted by a research journal. Later, a journalist reads that research journal and writes an article with the bold headline, "Omega-3 Makes People Happy."

Let's say in another study, the same procedure is followed, but two months later, the research participants report no change in their level of happiness. That's a boring result, therefore, it doesn't get accepted by a research journal. Because it doesn't get accepted, journalists don't hear about it. Therefore, there's no corresponding article suggesting that maybe omega-3 doesn't actually have a significant effect on happiness.

When looking at all omega-3 studies—not just those accepted by research journals—it becomes clear that the advertised effects of omega-3 are not as great as those otherwise suggested.

But still—those who are observed to consume more omega-3 are significantly less likely to get depression. Why can't studies experimentally replicate this observational effect?

There are three guesses why ...

One, folks who eat more fish are also more likely to do other things that contribute to happiness, like exercise, eat less trans fat, or spend more time socializing (not an unreasonable assumption, when one considers the types of cultures that have fish as a staple in their diet).

Two, omega-3 supplements are somehow different than eating actual fish.

Three, those who are genetically less likely to develop depression have a greater need for (and therefore consumption of) omega-3 fatty acids.

Whichever of these three hypotheses is actually are true, the underlying result is clear. Fish is healthy and useful to eat. But the jury is still out on the happiness benefits of taking omega-3 supplements.

Overall, omega-3 has been proven to promote heart health, so taking it can at least become an important health habit, even if there is conflicting evidence on its correlation to improving happiness. If you'd like to add this supplement to your diet, read my article on developgoodhabits.com in which I review some of the better options in the market.[285]

More Information

- Omega-3 Fatty Acids for the Treatment of Depression: Systematic Review and Meta-analysis[286]

- Dietary Fat Intake and the Risk of Depression: The SUN Project[287]

285 https://www.developgoodhabits.com/omega-3-supplements/

286 http://europepmc.org/articles/PMC3625950/reload=0;jsessionid= 7I17L31irSctZmHZJrEA.58

287 https://journals.plos.org/plosone/article?id=10.1371/journal.pone .0016268

35. Smile (Even if You're Faking It)

Smile. If you're sad, it's a bad idea to pretend that you're happy. Suppressing negative thoughts and feelings backfires. But if you're not sad or angry ...

Fake a smile. It'll make you happier.

According to the facial feedback hypothesis, it isn't only that being happy or sad will make you smile or frown, respectively, but that smiling or frowning will make you happy or sad. Research suggests that this hypothesis is true—with a few caveats.

In one study,[288] participants were asked to hold a pencil in their mouth in a way that either activated the muscles involved with smiling, or which prevented those muscles from being activated. After being exposed to a happy video clip, those with the "forced smile" reported a temporary increase in mood four times larger than those without the "forced smile."

So how can you fake your body signals?

It's simple: put your negative thoughts on hold, and then smile.

Here's what I mean ...

The facial feedback hypothesis[289] suggests that our facial expressions influence our emotions. Here's an oversimplified example:

> Our spouse tells us they love us → emotion center A in the brain tells our facial muscles to form a smile → our facial

---

288 https://www.psychologytoday.com/us/blog/isnt-what-i-expected/201208/try-some-smile-therapy
289 http://en.wikipedia.org/wiki/Facial_feedback_hypothesis

muscles form a smile → emotion center B reads our face and sees a smile, and it generates positive emotion.

I'm sure this idea seems ridiculous to you. After all, why does the emotion center that generates positive emotion need to read our faces to determine our emotional state? Shouldn't it know itself?

Our brains are complicated. Let's just leave it at that. If it wasn't for multiple supporting studies, I wouldn't believe it either:

- In one study,[290] an fMRI scan was done of participants before and after they received a Botox injection. When asked to imitate angry facial expressions, participants showed less brain activation in the brain regions involved in emotional processing and experiencing after they had been injected with Botox.

- In another study, participants watched negative, neutral, and positive video clips (e.g., a comedy clip versus a clip of a man eating a live worm). After each clip, they were asked to report how positive or negative they felt (from −4 to 4). The subgroup that was instructed not to move their face had a 100% better response to the negative clips. In other words, when emotion center B did not detect a frown, it did not generate strong negative feelings.

So let's talk about what you can do to take action on this idea.

I don't know about you, but I am always tired after lunch. Always. So I'm making it a habit to do four things after I've finished eating:

1. Laughing for as long as I can

---

290   https://academic.oup.com/cercor/article/19/3/537/429135

2. Putting on some energetic music and bobbing my head

3. Sitting up straight with good posture

4. Smiling for at least 10 minutes, regardless of how tired I feel

You might be tempted to tuck away this "fake smile" trick to use on a rainy day, but the best way to make use of it is to incorporate it into your daily schedule. Scientists have not yet explored if faking a smile produces weaker or stronger results the more you do it, but I believe this activity is a skill, just like cultivating gratitude: **the more you do it, the stronger the benefits**.

So, pick a trigger and pick an action.

- As a trigger, you can use a time of day, a mood, a smell, or even a person.

- As an action, you can act happy, fake a smile, bob your head, hold a pencil with your teeth, or straighten your posture.

This activity will make you happier and more energetic; and, because of the way our brains work, you will associate that additional happiness and energy with your trigger, not with the action.

More Information

- How to Fake a Smile For Health and Happiness[291]

- 10 Hidden Benefits of Smiling[292]

- The Claim: A Fake Smile Can be Bad for Your Health[293]

- Duchenne smile, emotional experience, and autonomic reactivity: A test of the facial feedback hypothesis[294]

- The Voluntary Facial Action Technique: A Method to Test the Facial Feedback Hypothesis[295]

---

291 http://happierhuman.com/smile/

292 http://www.spring.org.uk/2011/06/10-hidden-benefits-of-smiling.php

293 https://www.nytimes.com/2011/02/22/health/22really.html?mtrref=www
.google.com&gwh=BF4878CC26119A896DEF72E76A3C28D5&gwt=pay

294 http://psycnet.apa.org/journals/emo/2/1/52/

295 http://link.springer.com/article/10.1007%2Fs10919-010-0098-6

PART 5:

FINDING HAPPINESS BY ELIMINATING BAD HABITS

36. Spend Less Time on Your Phone

People today use their phones for just about everything.

A 2018 report[296] created by Mary Meeker discovered that the average American is online for approximately six hours each day. We do this to keep in touch with the people in our social circle and family, to stay on top of what's happening in our community and around the globe, to shop, to learn, to be entertained, and to earn money. Our phones are good for just about everything now.

Furthermore, data from a Flurrymobile study[297] reveals that American consumers use their phones five hours a day on average. For that number of hours, the top three app categories users spent time on were—in descending order—social media (Facebook), entertainment media (music, videos, etc.), and messaging.

Those five hours per day are equivalent to 150 hours per week, or 1,825 hours per year. That's roughly 2.5 months that people spend time on their phones annually!

As you read this, you'll realize that those hours you spend using your mobile phone could have been spent in a more meaningful way. So in this happiness habit, I will make the case for you to lessen the time you spend on your phone.

First, let's talk about the disadvantages of excessive phone use.

Despite the many benefits[298] of having a smartphone, there are

---

296   https://www.kleinerperkins.com/perspectives/internet-trends-report -2018

297   https://flurrymobile.tumblr.com/post/157921590345/us-consumers-time -spent-on-mobile-crosses-5

298   https://itstillworks.com/benefit-having-smartphone-1611.html

a lot of disadvantages as well. Perhaps the greatest negative effect is that **excessive smartphone use deteriorates the quality of your relationships with loved ones**.

A recent study[299] reveals that the average adult now checks his or her phone almost 50 times per day, regardless if that person is alone or with company.

Do you know that there's now a buzzword for the act of ignoring other people by paying more attention to your mobile phone?

The term is phubbing[300] (the habit of snubbing someone by looking at your phone during a conversation).

Excessive phone use also enhances your fear of missing out and lessens your feelings of satisfaction with your own life.

We are accountable for our actions, and it's good to recognize the negative impact of our constant use of mobile devices. However, this compulsive use of our phones is not entirely our fault.

You mean it's not my fault I'm so addicted to my phones?

The short answer is no.

Let me explain.

In his ground-breaking book Hooked: How to Build Habit-Forming Products,[301] Nir Eyal shares four steps guaranteed to form habits to hook consumers' interests and convince them to use a

---

299   https://www2.deloitte.com/us/en/pages/technology-media-and -telecommunications/articles/global-mobile-consumer-survey-us-edition.html
300   https://www.washingtonpost.com/news/inspired-life/wp/2017/10/13/are -you-phubbing-right-now-what-it-is-and-why-science-says-its-bad-for-your -relationships/?noredirect=on&utm_term=.4130f2b7f981
301   https://arkenea.com/blog/how-to-hook-mobile-app-users-insights-from -nir-eyals-hooked/

product over and over—pretty much keeping them addicted to the product.

Designers have applied the fundamentals of Eyal's work in the creation of apps for mobile phones. So far, the strategy works really well in keeping us, well, *hooked*.

Here are the four fundamental techniques that these companies use to keep you coming back for more:

1. The **external trigger** prompts users to choose the next step, and the **internal trigger** takes into account the user's current emotional state, perception, needs, and desires.

2. The **action** is the minimal desirable behavior that a user must do to get the perceived reward.

3. The **rewards** are the sense of accomplishment in achieving something by using the app, such as games, social rewards (e.g., the number of "likes" on Facebook), and the information one acquires about top-rated establishments from apps like Yelp.

4. The **investment** that users put in through effort, money, content, or emotional commitment guarantees future rewards and increases the user-experience value of an app the more frequently it's used.

Pretty scary stuff, right?

The simple truth is that technology companies are financially incentivized to keep you coming back for more. So it's up to *you* to recognize this fact and to build habits into your day that fight against this addictive technology.

Here are four suggestions to help you make this happen:

1. **Track your phone usage with an app.** Apps like Moment[302] for iPhones and Quality Time[303] for Android help you monitor your smartphone usage. Their features include monitoring access frequency, tracking the number of hours spent on the phone, and providing an optional reminder if you go over the limit of the allotted time you've set for yourself to use your mobile device.

2. **Plan how to productively use your newly freed time.** Cutting down on excessive phone use is a smart move. Nevertheless, you must replace this free time with productive activities, lest you'd be tempted to just sit and binge on movie-streaming sites. Perhaps now is a good time to work on scratching things off your bucket list.

3. **Do not sleep with your phone.** When you've had a hard day, you'll be tempted to seek solace from old habits such as mindlessly using your phone. Keeping your phone as far away from the bedroom as possible guarantees you won't be sucked into that easy escape from stress. And if you feel like you *need* the alarm feature on your phone in the morning? Invest in something called an "alarm clock." Yes, people still use these things.

4. **Delete your social media apps.** This seems like a cold-turkey approach, but this move doesn't mean you should forgo social media use for good. We know social media use is one of the most notorious time sucks on the phone. Try using the computer if you must go online and check on your friends' tweets, likes, posts, and tags.

Remember that your goal is to become happier. So don't think

---

302   https://inthemoment.io/
303   http://www.qualitytimeapp.com/

that taking extended periods of time off from your phone is deprivation. Instead, it's a simple habit that will help you free up the mental bandwidth to focus on the other enjoyable activities that life has to offer.

37. Spend Less Time Online

Similar to spending too much time on your phone, **greater Internet usage is correlated with unhappiness**.

In fact, in one study tracking 170 people during their first two years online,[304] "greater use of the Internet was associated with declines in participants' communication with family members in the household, declines in the size of their social circle, and increases in their depression and loneliness."

Another study[305] found that the impact of Internet use depended on how it was used. Extraverts were likely to use the Internet as a tool to strengthen the quantity and quality of their relationships. As a result, a year after getting Internet access, they reported being happier, more socially connected, and less lonely.

On the other hand, introverts given access to the Internet were likely to spend less time socializing—rather than instant messaging or emailing, they read articles or played online games. As a result, they reported being less happy, more lonely, less socially connected, and less confident.

Across both of these studies, heavy use of the Internet was correlated with an increase in levels of stress, perhaps because time spent online took away from time required for other things, like work.

The Internet is an amazing tool. I—and many people—love all that it has to offer. But you can also increase your happiness if

---

304   https://www.ncbi.nlm.nih.gov/pubmed/9841579
305   http://kraut.hciresearch.org/sites/kraut.hciresearch.org/files/articles/kraut02-paradox-revisited-16-20-2.pdf

you decrease the time you spend online, choosing to socialize with people face to face instead.

When scientists randomly pinged people throughout the day and asked them what they were doing and how they were feeling, socializing ranked #2 in activities that made them feel happiest, second only to sex.

And if you use the Internet as a tool to become a more informed citizen ... well, do so in moderation. If you value your imaginary ability to affect national politics more than your happiness, go ahead and spend hours a day reading the news. Some people actually create change, but for the 99% who don't, a few tidbits of information are enough to get by.

If you'd like to cut down on your Internet usage, here are a few strategies you can use to make that happen.

Monitor your Internet usage time.

Similar to phone usage, one of the simplest ways to cut down on your screen time is to start by monitoring how much time you *actually* spend online. To get started, use one of the apps on this page to track your Internet time.[306]

Furthermore, monitor how long it takes you to do each task, and record exactly what you did. Then determine if the activity was truly necessary. You'd be surprised at how much time you actually spend on necessary versus unnecessary online activities.

Block your access to favorite time-sink websites.

While it may feel ironic to use technology to stop you from

---

306   https://www.huffingtonpost.com/entry/technology-time-management_us
_5819ee11e4b0cb89fdff2a6d

using technology, this is where we are today. To increase your productivity while you are online, use apps that block your go-to sites.[307] This will lessen the temptation to jump over to these sites if the task at hand is challenging or undesirable.

Doing this will help curb your temptation to get on social media or check the latest entertainment news. You can control these apps so they only block your chosen websites during certain parts of the day or for a certain amount of time so you know exactly the kind of time you have to complete your work.

If your task calls for using a computer, do it immediately.

Whether it's conducting research for a school project or sending work emails, finish these tasks as soon as possible. Get all of the information you need from the Internet in the beginning so you don't have to get back on.

If you know you will have to get on the computer, you may be tired of doing your work by the time you actually get online. This feeling will tempt you to take a break, which could turn into hours of mindlessly browsing the Internet. Do all of your computer work at the beginning of your project when your motivation is high.

When working, avoid using your phone.

Due to smartphones, it is now very easy to access the Internet. To stop wasting time online, put away your phone (or switch to silent or airplane mode) when you are working or studying. Make sure you are unable to see or hear any notifications that come

---

307   https://www.theguardian.com/technology/2018/jan/27/mobile-phone -addiction-apps-break-the-habit-take-back-control

up. Keep your phone in another room or zipped up in your bag so it's out of sight and you aren't tempted to check it.

With your phone out of the way, you can concentrate more fully on the job at hand. After you do this for a while, you will actually find it quite liberating because you will see the amount of work you're able to get done and realize that you really didn't miss anything online in the process of being productive.

Psychologist Adam Alter explains in a TED Talk[308] why our gadgets make us feel unhappy and gives suggestions on how to live a richer, more meaningful life.

Seek professional help.

The problem with any type of addiction is that it can be difficult to determine when a hobby has taken hold of your life. But if you can't seem to stick to the boundaries you've set and you are spending more time online than you are with real people, it may be time to seek professional help.

Recently, Internet addiction has become a cause for concern in clinical psychiatry. If the effects of excessive Internet use are severely impacting your personal life, if you feel you can't live without the Internet, you should seek professional intervention.[309]

No matter how you decide to spend your time, try to limit your screen time as much as possible so you can live out in the real world. It may be tough to do at first, but once you realize how great life is when you're not on the Internet, you will be thankful that you made the decision to cut back.

---

308   https://www.ted.com/talks/adam_alter_why_our_screens_make_us_less _happy

309   https://www.ncbi.nlm.nih.gov/pmc/articles/PMC4804263/

More Information

- 13 Ways to Spend Less Time Online and Reclaim Your Real Life[310]

- The More Time We Spend Online, the Less Time We Spend Working[311]

- How to Spend Less Time on the Computer[312]

- Internet paradox: A social technology that reduces social involvement and psychological well-being?[313]

- Internet Paradox Revisited[314]

- A Survey Method for Characterizing Daily Life Experience: The Day Reconstruction Method[315]

310   http://www.marksdailyapple.com/13-ways-to-spend-less-time-online
-and-reclaim-your-real-life/#ixzz2mx4lOXxY
311   http://blogs.hbr.org/2013/10/the-more-time-we-spend-online-the-less
-time-we-spend-working/
312   http://www.wikihow.com/Spend-Less-Time-on-the-Computer
313   http://psycnet.apa.org/psycinfo/1998-10886-001
314   http://kraut.hciresearch.org/sites/kraut.hciresearch.org/files/articles
/kraut02-paradox-revisited-16-20-2.pdf
315   https://www.ncbi.nlm.nih.gov/pubmed/15576620

38. Spend Less Time on Facebook (and Other Social Media Sites)

Check just once a day. Press the x button after 10 minutes, rather than 30 minutes. Stalk two, rather than 10 people.

It's easy to experience unhappiness if you're constantly looking at snippets of your friends' lives and feeling like you're missing out.

The average American spends almost 90 minutes a day on social networks. Having a tool that makes socializing easier is great. However, overconsumption of social networking is correlated with depression, lower life satisfaction, and envy.

There are a few reasons excess use of Facebook can be harmful. The largest is that time spent on Facebook is less time spent socializing face to face. Talking to someone in person causes the release of a number of positive chemicals, creating feelings of happiness and reducing stress. The effect of communication through Facebook on releasing those happy chemicals is muted.

Likewise, Facebook envy is real.

On Facebook, people generally post pictures of themselves at their best—smiling at a party, relaxing on the beach, sharing some happy news, and so on. One might think seeing all this awesomeness would be uplifting, but often, it isn't. One reason being rich can have such a small impact on happiness is because happiness equals reality minus expectations.

Our expectations are mostly defined by our social group. If all of our friends are rich, we expect that we too should be rich. On Facebook, because we share mostly the positives of our lives, we create unreasonable expectations for others to live up to. This is why one-third of Facebook users report feeling one or more negative emotions after a session of using Facebook.

Unfortunately, Facebook is addictive. Our brains judge social information to be extremely valuable. At one time, when said information was scarce, it was valuable. Now it's not. Nevertheless, the desire to get as much social information as possible remains.

(**Side note:** I'm not picking on Facebook here. The same rules apply to *any* social media website where users spend an excessive amount of time, like Snapchat, Instagram, Twitter, or other flavor of the month.)

So if you'd like to reduce your social media time, here are seven quick suggestions:

1. **Lessen your memberships in social media networks.** Do you really need a membership to 15 different social media platforms, when eight of those function essentially the same way? Limiting your membership to different sites reduces the clutter in your newsfeed and helps you spend less time on social media overall.

2. **Turn off your notifications.** Wean yourself from being overly saturated with social media news by making it a point to turn off notifications. This ensures you don't get tempted to check your phone every time an alert pops up. Disable pop-up notifications through your phone settings. For computers, you might have to install a browser extension that blocks newsfeed alerts.

3. **Monitor the time you spend on social media.** Being mindful of the time you spend on social platforms is the beginning

of breaking this time-wasting habit. Set up a timer every time you log in to Facebook or other social media sites. Determine beforehand how many minutes (e.g., 20 minutes max) you'll spend on that session. Log off when the time is up.

4. **Consider social media as a tool.** If you're working to get more exposure for your business, or if you wish to develop more meaningful connections with people who share your interests, being on social media can help further your goals. By utilizing your networks in a productive way, social media ceases to be a meaningless time sink.

5. **Uninstall social media apps from your phone.** Let's face it: We're only logged in to Facebook all day because we've convinced ourselves that our newsfeed holds meaningful information. It's a major distraction, especially if we can easily access our accounts through our smartphones. By removing Facebook, Twitter, Snapchat, etc., from your phone, you become less distracted. Log in only through the computer, and still set a timer for yourself to ensure you don't spend too much time in there.

6. **Develop a "Do it now!" habit.** Oftentimes, we procrastinate by spending too much time checking our Facebook newsfeed in order to delay accomplishing something we don't actually want to do (i.e., responsibilities). Get it done now! Develop the habit of finishing your tasks before diving into your account.

7. **Keep in touch the old-school way.** Use your phone to actually call a friend or family member. Speak with them and find out how they are doing. Share some news from your life as well. Another way to keep in touch is to actually drop by and call on the person at their place. Get

back to your roots. Re-live memories. It serves as a more meaningful way to connect.

Always remember this:

Facebook and other social media sites are specifically designed to keep you coming back for more ... like a drug dealer.

Your job is to recognize this fact and build systems into your life that allow you to resist these temptations.

More Information

- Facebook Envy: How Cruising Can Kill Self Esteem[316]

- Facebook Envy: How The Social Network Affects Our Self-Esteem[317]

- Facebook Study Says Envy Is Rampant On The Social Network[318]

- "They Are Happier and Having Better Lives than I Am": The Impact of Using Facebook on Perceptions of Others' Lives[319]

- The Impact of Social Media on Children, Adolescents, and Families[320]

- Envy on Facebook: A Hidden Threat to Users' Life Satisfaction?[321]

---

316   http://www.huffingtonpost.com/wendy-sachs/facebook_b_1262681.html
317   http://www.wbur.org/2013/02/20/facebook-perfection
318   http://www.wbur.org/2013/02/20/facebook-perfection
319   http://connection.ebscohost.com/c/articles/71528600/they-are-happier
-having-better-lives-than-am-impact-using-facebook-perceptions-others-lives
320   http://pediatrics.aappublications.org/content/127/4/800.full
321   http://karynemlira.com/wp-content/uploads/2013/01/Envy-on
-Facebook_A-Hidden-Threat-to-Users%E2%80%99-Life.pdf

- "Facebook Depression?" Social Networking Site Use and Depression in Older Adolescents[322]
- Social Networking Eats Up 3+ Hours Per Day For The Average American User[323]

322   http://www.jahonline.org/article/S1054-139X(12)00209-1/abstract
323   http://www.marketingcharts.com/wp/interactive/social-networking-eats -up-3-hours-per-day-for-the-average-american-user-26049/

39. Don't Watch Too Much TV

Watching TV is fun. But does watching TV make us happy? Yes, but only in small amounts.

Like we discussed in habit #30 ("Buy Many Small Things"), **the size of your desire for something has little relation to the amount of happiness that thing will actually bring**.

A study mentioned in the *Handbook of Research Methods and Applications in Happiness and Quality of Life*[324] found that socializing was more enjoyable than watching TV as much as watching TV was more enjoyable than working. It's that big of a difference.

Taking data from 42,000 people from 22 countries, the study concluded that excessive TV viewers have lower life satisfaction. No surprise. The average American watches almost four hours of TV a day. Every hour spent watching TV is an hour not spent socializing, exercising, building self-esteem, or having sex.

In addition, there is a correlation between time spent watching TV and both your level of anxiety and your level of material aspirations. The second is particularly worrisome. When reality doesn't match up to the perfection, adventure, and romance that TV suggests our lives ought to have, unhappiness ensues.

Even more troubling, couples who keep a TV in the bedroom have 50% less sex than those that don't.

---

324   https://www.amazon.com/Handbook-Research-Applications-Happiness -Handbooks/dp/1783471166

TV exploits two biological principles to reliably create good feelings:

One: We are conditioned to conserve energy whenever possible. That is why, as our default, we sit rather than stand, and stand rather than exercise. TV conserves. Doubly so, in fact; TV rests both mind and body. What the body wants it makes enjoyable.

Two: We are conditioned to seek novelty whenever it is reasonably safe and efficient to do so. TV is both. Dopamine is released when we are exposed to new sounds, new images, new people, and new drama. TV provides all four.

Fortunately, you don't have to be a slave to your TV. In fact, you have three basic options to either completely eliminate this habit or minimize your overall usage:

Option 1: Wean yourself off TV.

By decreasing the amount of time you spend watching TV instead of going cold turkey, you're giving yourself time to adjust. You can start this by being very selective about what you choose to watch.

One of the reasons you may want to stop watching television is that the programs that come on aren't any good in the first place. If this is the case, don't replace what is airing on TV with other videos like reruns of shows you have seen before or programs that you don't truly enjoy. Instead, when you do choose to watch TV, try to *find something that is worth your time*. Watch a show that will teach you something, or watch classic movies. Increase your standards.

As you *do* watch these more purposeful shows, **keep a record of**

how much time you spend in front of the TV. Commit to reducing the number of hours each week, and use a timer if you need to so you can track how long you've been watching. If you know you only have a set amount of time to watch TV, you will be more likely to enjoy it and watch something that is actually worth your time.

Another part of watching TV with good intentions is to **not start watching new shows**. When you're trapped in a world of television, *everything* may start to seem like something you *need* to watch. Friends may breathlessly tell you how great a new series is and invite you over to start watching it with them.

You can get hooked on the "next best show" out there that everyone is talking about in the office, but if you don't even watch the first episode, you will have no interest in the con-versation. As time goes by, you'll notice that you either stop watching TV completely or only watch very specific things that don't eat up a lot of your time.

Weaning yourself off TV may also involve **dedicating a place and a time for it, and sticking to your rules**. Designate "screen-free" areas of your house, such as the kitchen, dining room, and bedroom. Applying a complete screen ban to these areas will prevent you from watching TV on your smartphone, DVD player, etc. as a substitute. Additionally, you can designate a specific day for TV watching.

If you don't want to stop watching TV completely, choose a day and a specified number of hours you can watch TV. You can even use it to reward yourself *if* you stick to the rules.

Option 2: Completely stop watching TV.

Quitting cold turkey is not for everybody, but if you're dedicated to making a positive change, this might be the right way for you. This will be difficult at first, especially if you tend to turn the television on out of habit and keep it running in the background. But it will get easier as time goes on.

Start by cutting off your access to TV. Cancel your cable TV subscription and your online streaming subscriptions. Remove the TVs from your home and the apps on your phone you use to watch videos. Sell, donate, or give away anything you can. Get rid of any temptations to watch TV or any reminders that television is an option for a pastime.

Replace this activity by **socializing with like-minded people who don't watch TV** either. This will take away the temptation to watch television, and it will also help you get accustomed to living like other people who avoid watching television. It won't take long for you to pick up on the more positive hobbies they enjoy and start adopting this new lifestyle.

To keep your mind off television shows, make sure to **unfollow social media accounts and other online platforms that are dedicated to TV shows**. Since you are no longer watching TV, you don't need to keep up with the latest gossip or news about the characters on the show—whether it is the real life of the actor or actress playing the character or their storyline in the plot of the show.

Instead of wasting hours watching TV, spending time on hobbies can help you truly relax and explore your talents.

Option 3: Substitute TV with a healthy habit.

Another approach is to replace watching TV with other healthier activities. It's not that difficult to find other things to do instead of watching TV.[325]

We have covered a variety of tactics on how to spend your free time throughout this book. So if you're looking for something to do, I suggest starting with habit #31 ("Enjoy a Hobby") and/or reviewing my article on 101 new skills you can learn.[326]

More Information

- 10 Reasons to Watch Less Television[327]
- Watch More TV; It Makes You Happy![328]
- Does watching TV make us happy?[329]
- A Survey Method for Characterizing Daily Life Experience: The Day Reconstruction Method[330]

---

325 https://www.developgoodhabits.com/things-to-do-instead-of-watching-tv/

326 https://www.developgoodhabits.com/new-skills-to-learn/

327 http://www.becomingminimalist.com/ten-reasons-to-watch-less-television/

328 http://happierhuman.com/tv/

329 http://www.ub.uni-koeln.de/ssg-bwl/archiv1/2009/99943_watching_tv_happy.pdf

330 https://www.ncbi.nlm.nih.gov/pubmed/15576620

40. Don't Watch Porn

Watching porn may seem harmless, but it's not.

Porn is not harmless. Evidence shows that regular porn consumption reduces relationship satisfaction.

Considering that relationship satisfaction is one of the strongest components of happiness, that's concerning. So if you're not convinced about the dangers, I *highly* recommend you read "Start here: Evolution has not prepared your brain for today's porn,"[331] or watch Gary Wilson's Ted Talk, "The great porn experiment"[332] on the effects of regular porn consumption. Either one will explain the idea better than I can.

One of the major issues with porn is how it releases dopamine, ultimately causing your reward circuitry to go astray.

Dopamine is the neurochemical of pleasure and motivation. Does thinking about time alone with your significant other create excitement? That's dopamine. Does thinking about a new car, house, or promotion create excitement? That's dopamine.

Thousands of years ago, dopamine drove us toward activities that ensured our survival and the propagation of our genes. Our bodies weren't designed for our modern-day environment of erotic abundance.

Porn releases so much dopamine that it desensitizes us. There's a reason that Men's Porn Use is Linked to Unhappy Relationships,[333]

---

331   http://www.yourbrainonporn.com/doing-what-you-evolved-to-do
332   http://www.youtube.com/watch?v=wSF82AwSDiU
333   http://www.livescience.com/20684-porn-relationships.html

but I think it has more to do with sensitization than self-esteem, as that study suggests.

Let's keep it simple:

If you can control your porn consumption (that is, abstain for a month if you wanted to), you're probably fine. If you can't, that probably means you're at least partially addicted.

More Information

- The Great Porn Experiment[334]

- Start here: Evolution has not prepared your brain for today's porn[335]

- Ditch Porn—It's Playboy on (Dopamine Draining) Steroids[336]

- Pornified: How Pornography Is Transforming Our Lives, Our Relationships, and Our Families[337]

- Pornography's Impact on Sexual Satisfaction[338]

---

334 https://www.youtube.com/watch?v=wSF82AwSDiU

335 http://www.yourbrainonporn.com/doing-what-you-evolved-to-do

336 http://happierhuman.com/porn/

337 https://www.amazon.com/Pornified-Pornography-Damaging
-Relationships-Families/dp/0805081321

338 http://onlinelibrary.wiley.com/doi/10.1111/j.1559-1816.1988.tb00027
.x/abstract

41. Don't Check Your Portfolio All the Time

Unless you're a Wall Street trader with ultra-low latency, direct market access, and an army of analysts or a patient genius like Warren Buffett, active investing is a negative-sum game.

On the other hand, the person who invests in an index fund and then goes to sleep will, on average, outperform the active investor.

The folks who are beating the index fund are well-resourced, obsessive hedge fund managers and caffeine-fueled overworked Wall Street analysts, not your five-hours-a-week hobbyist.

Frequently checking your stock portfolio will also decrease your well-being. There are three ways in which frequently checking your portfolio can hurt.

First, we like to feel in control. We don't have control over stock prices; if we did, we'd be billionaires. What draws us to checking over and over again is the allure of novelty. We have a vestigial desire to acquire as much information as possible, even if it's not actually helpful.

Second, we feel our losses more strongly than we feel our gains. They'll be stronger in intensity and will last longer. For example, if a friend calls us beautiful, we're likely to be extra happy for a few minutes or hours. On the other hand, if a friend calls us ugly, it's likely to affect us for the whole day, perhaps even longer.

On average, the value of a stock will increase by a few percentage points each year. The value investor who invests and then checks back a few years later is likely to see an increase. But this long-term increase is composed of tens of thousands of small bumps and jumps—both up and down.

Because we feel losses more strongly than gains, and because there will be almost as many decreases as increases, for many the net impact on their emotions will be negative.

Almost like an *addiction*.

Third, we get addicted to random rewards. If we knew exactly when we were going to get a new important email, we would check it at only those times. But we don't, so we check and check, over and over again.

Likewise with the stock market, stock prices are unpredictable. Sometimes the price goes down, sometimes it goes up. Because we don't know when it will go up, we check all the time, over and over again.

So if you'd like to cut down on some of your anxiety (and unhappiness), stop looking at your portfolio on a daily basis.

More Information

- Loss Aversion[339]
- Why Index Funds Beat Actively-Managed Funds[340]
- The Framing of Decisions and the Psychology of Choice[341]
- The Power of Reframing Incentives: Field Experiment on (Students') Productivity[342]

---

339   http://en.wikipedia.org/wiki/Loss_aversion
340   http://mutualfunds.about.com/od/Index-Investing/a/Why-Index-Funds
-Beat-Actively-Managed-Funds.htm
341   http://psych.hanover.edu/classes/cognition/papers/tversky81.pdf
342   http://www.scienpress.com/Upload/AMAE/Vol 3_2_2.pdf

42. Don't Vent Your Anger

The next time a car cuts you off, don't start screaming about the driver's mother. That seemingly harmless behavior is both destructive and within your control. Likewise with other areas of your life, like getting angry at customer service or at your spouse.

Venting is doubly counterproductive, making you less likely to get what you want *and* more likely to feel unhappy.

Although venting may feel good in the short-term, it is a myth that it actually works to "process" and lower your level of anger.

To illustrate this point, consider the following quote from "Catharsis," a great article on venting.[343] (And if you experience lots of anger, read the rest—it's brilliant!)

> Releasing sexual tension feels good. Throwing up when you are sick feels good. Finally getting to a restroom feels good. So, it seemed to follow, draining bad blood or driving out demons or siphoning away black bile to bring the body back into balance must be good medicine. Be it an exorcism or a laxative, the idea is the same: get the bad stuff out and you'll return to normal.
>
> It's drug-like, because there are brain chemicals and other behavioral reinforcements at work. If you get accustomed to blowing off steam, you become dependent on it.
>
> Common sense says venting is an important way to ease tension, but common sense is wrong. Venting—catharsis—is pouring fuel into a fire.

---

343   http://youarenotsosmart.com/2010/08/11/catharsis/

When we think about positive things, we become happy. When we think about negative things, we become unhappy. Likewise, when we act happy, perhaps by smiling, sitting up straight, or laughing, we become happier. More generally, if we focus on positive thoughts and behaviors, we become happy. If we focus on unhappy thoughts and behaviors, we become unhappy.

So when studies show that venting by punching a pillow increases, rather than decreases, levels of anger, the reason is clear: those people are refocusing the brain's attention on angry thoughts and angry actions, causing even more anger. The psychological concept of Freudian repression has been largely disproven.

That isn't to say you should do nothing when you experience anger. Self-help did get one thing right—anger does need to be dealt with. There are simply more effective ways to do so than yelling or punching, like relaxing, empathizing, and taking time for quiet reflection. Sound familiar? These are many of the strategies we've covered throughout this book.

More Information

- Catharsis[344]

- The Muddled Tracks of All Those Tears[345]

- Does Venting Anger Feed or Extinguish the Flame? Catharsis, Rumination, Distraction, Anger, and Aggressive Responding[346]

---

344   http://youarenotsosmart.com/2010/08/11/catharsis/

345   http://www.nytimes.com/2009/02/03/health/03mind.html?_r=2&

346   https://illinois.edu/lb/files/2009/03/26/9293.pdf

- Catharsis, Aggression, and Persuasive Influence: Self-Fulfilling or Self-Defeating Prophecies?[347]

---

347 http://www-personal.umich.edu/~bbushman/bbs99.pdf

43. Don't Ruminate

As we've discussed: Rumination is obsessive thinking about negative remarks about yourself, your actions, your past mistakes, or other negative events that happened in the past.

So if you find yourself ruminating, do whatever you can to escape. Focus your attention on more positive thoughts. Or, instead of replaying abstract worries over and over again, get specific and focus on problem-solving.

Rumination increases negative thinking, reduces problem-solving, erodes social support, and increases your risk of developing depression. In the ancestral environment, rumination was useful. If you were hungry and started ruminating about your lack of food, you could then go hunting or trading.

Now, many of the things we ruminate about are outside our control, turning what was once a useful psychological response into a harmful one. Ruminating about last night's date, about getting passed over for a promotion, over your faux pas, over an upcoming presentation—it won't help.

Rumination triggers a negative spiral. Ruminating makes you feel bad, which causes your mind to focus on anxieties and worries, which makes you feel bad, and so on.

Rumination is almost always unproductive. That's why you should look for ways to fight against these thought processes.

Some causes of rumination include:

- failure to manage emotions during early childhood
- having a history of physical, sexual, or emotional trauma

- example shown by parents who also have the tendency to ruminate

- individuals with perfectionist or overachieving personalities

And some ways to stop ruminating include purposefully finding a distraction to keep repetitive thoughts at bay; adjusting your life goals to make room for the imperfect and unexpected; learning to love and accept yourself for who and what you are at present; identifying the things that could trigger mental rumination; talking it out with a trusted person; and seeking professional help.

Bottom line: Rumination is another bad habit you can overcome by implementing many of the higher-level strategies we've covered in this book (i.e., mindfulness, meditation, and focusing on the present moment). You'll discover that the more you engage in these activities, the less time you'll have to dwell on the negative kind of thinking that causes rumination.

More Information

- Why Ruminating is Unhealthy and How to Stop[348]
- Rethinking Rumination[349]

---

348 http://psychcentral.com/blog/archives/2011/01/20/why-ruminating-is-unhealthy-and-how-to-stop/
349 http://drsonja.net/wp-content/themes/drsonja/papers/NWL2008.pdf

44. Don't Fantasize

Fantasizing in excess has two negative effects: it makes you less likely to actually change your life, and it can raise your expectations in harmful ways.

A simple truth:

Images of success can take the place of *actual* action. The fantasy replaces reality.

Check out "Why Generation Y Yuppies Are Unhappy"[350] for the best illustration of how high expectations can harm happiness. The article applies to everyone; as we acquire more in life, our fantasies get progressively more and more ambitious. Desire for improvement is good, but happiness is the difference between reality and our expectations.

If our expectations increase in tandem with reality, our level of happiness will stay unchanged. This is what usually happens, and it's why happiness over a person's lifetime looks more like a flat line rather than a constant march upward (which we covered in the section about the hedonic treadmill.).

Another negative consequence of fantasizing is that it reduces goal attainment. Positive visualization feels good, but so does cocaine. Neither is much good for long-term motivation.

The Law of Attraction is bogus. It's effective at making you feel good temporarily, but at the cost of long-term action and well-being.

---

350   The best illustration of how high expectations can harm happiness is this article –

Positivity is healthy and productive. But raising expectations without corresponding action decreases long-term well-being. In tests, the average person who followed the Law of Attraction saw a reduction in goal attainment. On the flip side, those who followed mental contrasting, a process that involves some focus on negative thoughts, saw an increase in goal attainment.

Instead of living in a fantasy world, one of the best strategies you can implement is to take <u>every</u> objective you'd like to reach in life and turn it into a goal.

Sounds simplistic, right?

Well, as we've discussed, many people would rather fantasize about what their lives *could be* like rather than take action. **You, on the other hand, can stop fantasizing by using a strategy that's commonly known as S.M.A.R.T. goal setting**.

It stands for:

- **S**pecific
- **M**easurable
- **A**ttainable
- **R**elevant
- **T**ime-bound

Specific

Specific goals answer your six "W" questions:

"Who?"

"What?"

"Where?"

"When?"

"Which?"

"Why?"

When you can identify each element, you'll know which tools (and actions) are required to reach a goal:

- Who is involved?
- What do you want to accomplish?
- Where will you complete the goal?
- When do you want to do it?
- Which requirements and constraints might get in your way?
- Why are you doing it?

Specificity is important because when you reach these milestones (date, location, and objective), you'll know for certain you have achieved your goal.

Measurable

Measurable goals are defined with precise times, amounts, or other units—essentially anything that measures progress toward a goal.

Creating measurable goals makes it easy to determine if you have progressed from point A to point B. Measurable goals also help you figure out whether you're headed in the right direction. Generally, a measurable goal statement answers questions starting with *How*: "How much?" "How many?" and "How fast?"

Attainable

Attainable goals stretch the limits of what you think is possible. While they're not impossible to complete, they're often challenging and full of obstacles. The key to creating an attainable goal is to look at your current life and set an objective that seems *slightly* beyond your reach. That way, even if you fail, you still accomplish something of significance.

Relevant

Relevant goals focus on what you truly desire. They are the exact opposite of inconsistent or scattered goals. They are in harmony with everything that is important in your life, from success in your career to happiness with the people you love.

Time-Bound

Time-bound goals have specific deadlines. You are expected to achieve your desired outcome before a target date. Time-bound goals are challenging and grounding. You can set your target date for today, or you can set it for a few months, weeks, or years from now. The key to creating a time-bound goal is to set a deadline you'll meet by working backward and developing habits (more on this later).

Examples of S.M.A.R.T. Goals

A S.M.A.R.T. goal is clear and well-defined. There is no doubt about the result you want to achieve. At its deadline, you'll know if you *have* or *haven't* achieved a particular goal.

As an example, here are S.M.A.R.T. goals related to seven core values that many people have:

1. **Career:** "I will acquire five new projects for my web design consultancy through referrals, networking, and social media marketing campaigns within three months."

2. **Family:** "I will strengthen my bond with my family by taking them for a vacation at least once in six months. This will be accomplished by setting aside two hours each month to plan our family trip."

3. **Marriage:** "I will identify three things I really love about my partner and tell her about them on Friday night. This will be done by scheduling a 30-minute block on Tuesday so I can reminisce about all the good times we've shared together."

4. **Spirituality:** "I will take five minutes each day to give thanks for everything that's good in my life. I will develop this habit by setting aside time right before my lunch to remember what's important."

5. **Artistry:** "I will dedicate three hours every week to learn and practice watercolor painting. This will be done by eliminating unimportant habits, like watching TV."

6. **Finances:** "I will save 10% of every paycheck and invest it in index funds through Vanguard."

7. **Fitness:** "I will work out a minimum of 30 minutes a day, three days a week by December 31."

Hopefully, these seven examples give you an idea of how to create S.M.A.R.T. goals that lead to a balanced life.

So my challenge to you:

Rather than live in a fantasy world, look for the specific steps to make your goals happen and turn them into an action plan.

Not only will you reduce a negative habit that might limit your happiness, you'll also get more satisfaction from working toward an outcome that will improve your life.

More Information

- Why Generation Y Yuppies Are Unhappy[351]

- The Myth of Inspiration—Why Feeling Excited Isn't Enough[352]

- Self-regulation strategies improve self-discipline in adolescents: Benefits of mental contrasting and implementation intentions[353]

- Mental contrasting facilitates academic performance in school children[354]

- When planning is not enough: Fighting unhealthy snacking habits by mental contrasting with implementation intentions (MCII).[355]

- Mental contrasting instigates goal pursuit by linking obstacles of reality with instrumental behavior

351   http://www.waitbutwhy.com/2013/09/why-generation-y-yuppies-are-unhappy.html

352   http://happierhuman.com/the-myth-of-inspiration/

353   http://www.tandfonline.com/doi/abs/10.1080/01443410.2010.506003#.UqEVXsRDutw

354   https://link.springer.com/article/10.1007/s11031-011-9222-0

355   http://onlinelibrary.wiley.com/doi/10.1002/ejsp.730/abstract?systemMessage=Wiley+Online+Library+will+be+disrupted+on+7+December+from+10%3A00-15%3A00+GMT+%2805%3A00-10%3A00+EST%29+for+essential+maintenance&userIsAuthenticated=false&deniedAccessCustomisedMessage=

- Mental contrasting of a dieting wish improves self-reported health behavior[356]

- Mental contrasting and the self-regulation of helping relations[357]

- Self-regulation of commitment to reduce cigarette consumption: Mental contrasting of future with reality[358]

---

356 http://www.tandfonline.com/doi/abs/10.1080/08870446.2011.626038#.UqEVocRDutw

357 http://guilfordjournals.com/doi/abs/10.1521/soco.2010.28.4.490

358 http://www.tandfonline.com/doi/abs/10.1080/08870440903079448#.UqEVxcRDutw

45. Don't Use Positive Affirmations

A common recommendation in self-help books and TV shows for increasing self-esteem and happiness is to use positive affirmations—to repeat to oneself positive self-statements. For example, "I am a lovable person. I am making the right choices. I have every bit as much brightness to offer the world as the next person."

While *self*-affirmations are effective, *positive* affirmations are not. We aren't fooling anyone when we think we suck at something but repeat in our head that we're actually great at it.

Self-affirmations *are* effective. They involve writing or talking about personal qualities we know we have. Specifically, discussing how we tend to express those qualities, and why we think they're important. On the other hand, positive affirmations are a quick fix that doesn't work.

There are three reasons positive affirmations can and often do backfire.

The first reason is that thought suppression doesn't work. For example, in one study,[359] participants were told not to think about white bears. Then, they were instructed to ring a bell every time thoughts of a white bear intruded upon their mind. The results were clear and repeatable with more real-world examples—asking someone to avoid thinking about something actually increases *by an order of magnitude* how frequently they think those thoughts.

---

359   https://study.com/academy/lesson/the-white-bear-problem-ironic
-process-theory.html

So suggesting that someone should tell themselves, "I am beautiful" and should avoid thinking, "I am ugly" can have the opposite effect of increasing how likely they are to think to themselves that they are ugly.

The second reason is that our brains aren't stupid. If you don't actually think you're lovable, telling yourself you're lovable will bring to mind doubts that what you're telling yourself isn't genuine, which in turn will decrease rather than increase your self-esteem.

This is why studies suggest positive affirmations increase happiness and self-esteem among those who *already have* high self-esteem. For them, "I am beautiful and I will succeed" is believable. For those with low self-esteem, it's not, and so the affirmation actually decreases long-term self-esteem.

The third reason is that the use of positive affirmations carries the assumption that it's bad to think negative thoughts. Therefore, when a person does think negative thoughts, they will think worse of themselves—that only losers or unhappy people think negative thoughts. That's false. Everyone thinks negative thoughts every now and again. Or they will think themselves a failure for being unable to follow the program and keep negative thoughts away. That's unfortunate because negative thoughts can't be forced away by sheer force of will.

More Information

- Self-help books 'can have the opposite effect'[360]
- Should we re-think positive thinking?[361]
- The Power of Affirming Your Values[362]
- Benefits of Self-Affirmation[363]
- Self-Control Instantly Replenished by Self-Affirmation[364]
- Positive Self-Statements: Power for Some, Peril for Others[365]

360   http://www.telegraph.co.uk/health/healthnews/5735549/Self-help-books
-can-have-the-opposite-effect.html
361   http://www.psychologytoday.com/blog/regarding-self-regard/200903
/should-we-re-think-positive-thinking
362   https://serc.carleton.edu/sage2yc/musings/values.html
363   http://www.cmu.edu/homepage/health/2013/summer/benefits-of-self
-affirmation.shtml
364   http://www.spring.org.uk/2010/03/self-control-instantly-replenished-by
-self-affirmation.php
365   https://www.uni-muenster.de/imperia/md/content/psyifp/aeechterhoff
/wintersemester2011-12/seminarthemenfelderdersozialpsychologie/04_wood
_etal_selfstatements_psychscience2009.pdf

46. Don't Complain

Receiving social support and making your troubles understood feels great, but every time you complain, you're spreading negativity, putting yourself into victim mode, and improving your ability to find things to complain about in the future.

My advice?

If you feel the need to complain, try to complain in moderation.

The brain has the unfortunate tendency to focus on the negative. Complaining is almost never the most useful reaction to a circumstance—it is merely the most natural. For those who are happiest, that tendency has been flipped around.

Holding things in is no good, but dwelling on the negative is no better.

So if you'd like to eliminate this habit, here are a few suggestions to help you get started:

- **Change your perception of the situation.** Our brains oftentimes prefer to dwell on negativity.[366] Although challenging, when you encounter a less-than-favorable situation, rather than focusing on the negative, try to find the good in it. In this case, the practice of mindfulness is very helpful to keep yourself grounded in the present. See things for what they are and you will be complaining less.

- **Identify the things you are grateful for.** What are you thankful for today? When you name each thing, person, and situation that makes you feel grateful, you've started a positive habit that overcomes your tendency to complain.

366   https://en.wikipedia.org/wiki/Negativity_bias

You can write them down[367] to better reinforce the habit of gratefulness in your life. (Once again, we see that showing gratitude is an effective tool for increasing happiness.)

- **Avoid using complaints as a conversation starter.** Sometimes people fall into the habit of using complaints to begin conversations because it earns a higher reaction from the listeners. It's time to stop doing this. How about spreading some cheer by mentioning something positive when you initiate a conversation?

- **Accept imperfection.** As mentioned above, there are numerous situations in life that don't go as we expect. We will all go through pain, challenges, and suffering as long as we are alive. It is okay to experience hardship. We all encounter setbacks. What's important is to recognize that we're not the only ones who suffer.

- **Monitor what sets you off.** What triggers you to go on a long rant? Is it when you're on a water cooler break at work? Is it when your significant other is at home? Is it at a certain time of the day? Pay attention to situations that encourage you to voice your complaints, and avoid them as much as possible. If you cannot avoid being in a location that triggers your complaining tendencies, be extra vigilant about your words.

- **Become a force for positive actions.** To quote Gandhi, "Be the change that you wish to see in the world." If you are determined to stop complaining, you have the choice to speak up to stop someone else from doing it or stay quiet so as not to fan the flames of negativity. If you choose to speak up, do so in the most diplomatic way possible.

---

367   https://www.developgoodhabits.com/gratitude-journal-prompts/

- **Learn to distinguish between constructive criticism and a complaint.** It is appropriate to raise attention to an issue if a wrong is being committed. Analyze if the situation needs to be fixed or if it can be fixed. If it's neither of the two, avoid joining in the fray.

- **Discover what makes you happy.** What do you enjoy doing that makes you forget the passage of time? Discovering a new hobby or focusing on your interests will shift your attention from things you tend to complain about because you'll be engaging in "soul work." The happier you feel, the less time you'll spend complaining.

- **Take time to take care of yourself.** Even people with the highest positive outlook get worn down by stress. Take time out for self-care activities. This practice recharges you and helps you ward off the negativity that is usually the root of a complaining behavior.

It's perfectly normal to experience life challenges. And it's also normal to sometimes dwell in negative thinking. Stuff happens sometimes. That said, what's not normal is to constantly complain about every small setback in life. So if you find yourself consistently getting upset at everything, I recommend using some (or all) of the strategies outlined above.

More Information

- How to Complain Less[368]
- 10 Ways to Complain Less (and Be Happier)[369]

---

368   http://www.becomingminimalist.com/complain-less/
369   http://tinybuddha.com/blog/10-ways-to-complain-less-and-be-happier/

47. Don't Settle

In too many areas of our lives, after we've made enough progress to become comfortable, we stop learning, growing, and making changes.

Not only is this an unfortunate attitude, it can also lead to unhappiness. In fact, it's only by making a change that happiness can increase.

No change = stagnation = less happiness.

Most often, the focus of our change is in places that don't have a long-term impact—continuously switching careers or romantic partners, or buying new things, over and over again. That kind of behavior is based on compensation and novelty replacement.

At first, the object or the job or the person provides lots of novelty and joy. As time progresses, the novelty and, consequently, the joy decrease. To compensate, a new job or object or person is found. Bang, the novelty returns. Over time, the novelty decreases. To compensate, a new job or object or person is found. And so on, again and again.

This kind of behavior leads to stagnation. Instead, the focus of change ought to be in places where progress is cumulative, rather than replacement.

Having two close friends brings more happiness than having one close friend. Being in a romantic relationship with someone who is compassionate, zestful, and grateful as well as attractive, will bring more happiness than being in a romantic relationship with someone who is not those things but merely attractive.

Adding 30 minutes of exercise or meditation to your routine will increase your happiness for as long as you continue the practice.

At work, what defines the expert is not some innate strength or intelligence that most lack. Rather, it is an insatiable desire to continue learning and improving, well past the point most would have felt comfortable and stopped.

The same is true of happiness.

What defines the expert self-improver is an insatiable desire to continue making improvements to their life, well past the point most would have felt comfortable and stopped.

But remember, aim for cumulative improvement rather than novelty replacement. Although earning more money in order to purchase a larger house might seem like a cumulative improvement, psychologically, the impact is more of novelty replacement.

Finding another romantic partner because you've lost interest is novelty replacement. Investing in good relationship or attraction habits is cumulative improvement.

One five-year study of mid-level managers[370] found that those who frequently switched jobs were on average less satisfied than those who stayed at the same company. Although these switchers experienced a boost of satisfaction and enjoyment for the first few months of each new job, they subsequently experienced a large drop. Rather than finding ways of coping and improving the environment, they did the only thing they knew how: they switched to another job.

So, the lesson here? Be very selective about the important things

---

370   https://scholarworks.wmich.edu/cgi/viewcontent.cgi?article=1945& context=dissertations

in your life: Your friends, your job, your spouse, and how you spend your precious time. When you surround yourself with greatness, you'll feel inspired and, ultimately, happier.

48. Don't Be Passive

Make new friends. Try new things. Go to new places.

In short, don't be passive. When you live *passively*, you're relying on the world to make you happy.

On the other hand, when you live *actively*, you're relying on yourself to make you happy.

This mindset is especially crucial when it comes to meeting people.

There are three ways you can meet new people. One, someone introduces you. Two, someone walks up to you. Three, you walk up to someone. The first two are largely out of your control. The third isn't.

If you want to live an awesome life, you've got to be active. Don't count on luck to meet your future spouse or discover your life calling.

Some people complain that they don't have any passions in their life. When I ask them what they're trying, the response is usually "nothing." Don't let that be you; don't rely on luck to fill your life with awesomeness.

If you'd like to take a more active role in your happiness, here are a couple of ways to make that happen:

- **Take ownership of how you want life to unfold *for you*.** You cannot depend on other people to make things happen in your life. You must take the initiative to work toward the success you want.
- **Ask yourself why you want to succeed or reach a goal.** By

knowing your inner motivation for wanting something, you'll understand its importance in your life so you can have an inner compass as you work toward accomplishing it.

- **Expect that you will succeed.** And work toward that success each day.

- **Train yourself to speak in proactive language.** The way you speak is a reflection of how you see the world. So if you constantly say you have no choice over something or you can't do a thing, it means you think others have power over you or that you're powerless to affect your life. Stop surrendering your power. Try saying, "I choose ..." or "I prefer ..." as a reminder that you do have a choice on how things will be in your life.

- **When you encounter a problem, focus on finding the solution or best course of action.** Most people dwell on the problem and its negative consequences. Being proactive means going beyond these issues and actually searching for a way to fix the problem.

- **Surround yourself with people who inspire you and encourage you to achieve success.** Remember, they cannot do anything to give you success, but they can help push you toward the right path, especially on those days you feel like giving up on your goals.

- **Be honest with yourself.** If things are not working out the way you envisioned them, it's okay to tell yourself that. Don't make excuses during times when you're not making progress.

Yes, it takes more effort to be active than it does to be passive. There will be times when you might want to blame others for things going wrong. But when you take charge of your own future, you will experience more happiness than those who allow randomness to dictate the outcome of their lives.

49. Don't Be a Pushover

Communicate your preferences. Ask for what you want. Set boundaries. Be neither passive nor aggressive—be assertive.

Assertiveness increases self-esteem, empowers you to get your needs met, is correlated with relationship satisfaction, and reduces levels of stress. It should come as no surprise that assertiveness can lead to more happiness.

Nevertheless, most people are not as assertive as they would optimally be.

Whether that's because we were taught in school to shut up and be good sheep, or because we think we're doing the world a favor by being a pushover, assertiveness is uncommon. That's unfortunate because assertiveness is honesty—to ourselves and to others.

Assertiveness can mean many things, such as giving your opinion, actively disagreeing, making a request, saying no to a request, standing your ground, setting a boundary, or being decisive.

Here are a couple of strategies that can help you build the assertiveness habit:

- **Believe that you also have rights.** You have the right to voice your needs, opinions, beliefs, feelings, and thoughts.
- **Establish your personal boundaries.** Things that you commit to are your boundaries (family, hobbies, health, your spirituality, well-being), and these are usually compromised if you aren't assertive in maintaining the boundaries when encountering resistance.

- **Aim to be open and tactfully honest in your assertiveness.** Keep in mind that being assertive is not the same as being aggressive. Gently and respectfully express what you need to say.

- **Use a subtle, slow-paced tone, combined with some playfulness or humor.** A high-pitched tone is seen as a sign of insecurity. Also, veer away from using gruff tones, as this signals aggressiveness.

- **Keep eye contact when you communicate.** Smile slightly as you do so, crinkling the sides of your eyes to differentiate your eye contact from an aggressive stare. This does take practice to perfect, but once you do, you'll notice that people pay more attention to what you have to say.

- **Learn to say no.** When a request or opinion conflicts with your personal boundaries, stand up for yourself and politely refuse.

- **Do not wait for someone else to fix your problems for you.** If there is an issue that you're unhappy about in your life, take action to change it. And it's okay if you can't change things overnight, as long as you've taken the steps to change things.

- **Practice being assertive in small ways first.** Low-risk situations can help you feel comfortable about voicing your needs or opinions.

More Information

- How To Be Assertive[371]

- Being assertive: Reduce stress, communicate better[372]

- Facets of extraversion related to life satisfaction[373]

- An Investigation of Assertiveness and Satisfaction with Life among Malaysian Secondary School Students[374]

- Effect of assertiveness training on levels of stress and assertiveness experienced by nurses in Taiwan, Republic of China[375]

- Relationship satisfaction in women: a longitudinal case-control study about the role of breast cancer, personal assertiveness, and partners' relationship-focused coping[376]

371 http://www.artofmanliness.com/2013/02/12/how-to-be-assertive/

372 http://www.mayoclinic.com/health/assertive/SR00042

373 http://www.sciencedirect.com/science/article/pii/S0191886997001943

374 http://ijm.cgpublisher.com/product/pub.28/prod.1422

375 http://www.ncbi.nlm.nih.gov/pubmed/8056571

376 http://www.ncbi.nlm.nih.gov/pubmed/17999780

50. Drink Less Alcohol

Statistics say 7% of Americans are alcoholics. That's one out of every 13 adults. Depression can lead to alcoholism, but the relationship is stronger the other way around.

Alcohol increases your risk of developing depression by 190%.

Whether it's because alcohol is neurotoxic—causing damage to the brain—because alcoholism triples your chances of divorce, or because of the financial and social stress it can cause, alcoholism significantly reduces life satisfaction and happiness.

If you're a heavy drinker and you care about your happiness and the happiness of those around you, make dealing with your alcoholism a top priority.

One way to do this is to attend a local Alcoholics Anonymous (AA) meeting.[377] An important person in my life goes to these meetings, and I attend their yearly chip anniversary. So I can speak from personal experience when I highly recommend the value of these groups and the positive impact they can have on your life. AA can save your life—*if you're willing to do the steps.*

On the other hand, if you don't consider yourself to be a heavy drinker and you'd simply like to minimize the drinking habit, here are six ideas to limit your intake on a weekly basis:

1. **Transform a negative habit into a positive one.** You can choose[378] to drink a non-alcoholic beverage to replace the alcoholic one; or choose to exercise, take a walk, or have a piece of fruit instead of drinking.

---

377   https://www.aa.org/
378   https://www.rd.com/health/wellness/limit-alcohol/

2. **Stop keeping drinks inside the house.** This action helps you cut back on drinking because it takes extra effort to secure alcohol when you don't have any in the house.

3. **Measure out your drink.** If you're determined to cut back on drinking, measuring your shots can help you achieve your goal. Use a jigger spirit measure for single shots to monitor how many shots you're having. You'll soon realize that you quickly go way over the limit if you're not careful.

4. **Drink slowly.** If you happen to drink, do it slowly. Consuming your drink in a mindful way can make you appreciate it and allow you to enjoy it more without compelling you to guzzle.

5. **Have days when you completely abstain from alcohol.** Choose to have at least one or two days a week of not drinking any alcoholic beverage. Take note of improvements in your mood, your interaction with others, and your general well-being.

6. **Be kind to yourself.** Don't beat yourself up if you experience some setbacks in your goal to curb excessive drinking. Persistence is the key. Acknowledge the effort you're making to achieve a positive change in your life.

More Information

- Alcohol Abuse May Lead To Depression Risk, Rather Than Vice Versa[379]
- Alcoholism Statistics[380]
- Alcohol and Depression[381]
- Heavy Drinking Raises Risk of Divorce[382]
- Drink and Be Merry? Gender, Life Satisfaction, and Alcohol Consumption Among College Students[383]

---

379 http://www.medicalnewstoday.com/releases/140924.php

380 http://alcoholismstatistics.net/

381 http://www.webmd.com/depression/alcohol-and-depresssion

382 http://www.livescience.com/26884-heavy-drinking-raises-divorce.html

383 http://psycnet.apa.org/journals/adb/19/2/184/

51. Maybe Skip the Sugar

Water instead of soda. Fat instead of sugar. Apples instead of cookies.

A study of 263,925 people[384] showed that those drinking more than three cans of soda a day were 30% more likely to develop depression.

There are a number of different reasons to suggest that sugar lowers long-term mood.

First, sugar can cause energy spikes, which for a while will feel great but will then lead to a crash. Feeling sluggish and tired is a surefire way to get unhappy.

Second, large quantities of sugar are unhealthy and can cause certain chronic diseases, like diabetes.

Third, like porn, sugar is addictive and can cause downregulation of dopamine. Dopamine is the chemical of desire and excitement. Thinking about an upcoming party or something you want to do will cause you to release dopamine. Dopamine is what gets you out of bed, giving you the desire to go to work, hang out with friends, and learn new things.

Sugar is different. Sugar causes a surge of dopamine far in excess of normal. This surge builds your desire, so you consume again. Bam! Another surge. So you consume again, and again, and again.

To maintain homeostasis, your brain decreases its response to sugar so that you need to eat increasingly higher amounts to get

---

384   https://www.sciencedaily.com/releases/2013/01/130108162135.htm

the same response. With this now reduced response, it's possible that the person who eats only one or two sweets a week is getting an overall larger effect than the person who eats six every day.

The reason I made this strategy a "maybe" is because there are easier strategies available and because nutrition science is a mess. For example, in the study mentioned above, income is not controlled for. Why does that matter?

Some reports indicate folks most likely to drink lots of soda are those who are poor. Those who are poor are more likely to be unhappy and develop depression, for reasons that have nothing to do with their diet and consumption of sugar, like being unemployed or raising a child on their own.

To quit sugar, you must be prepared to build a new identity as someone who eats healthy and avoids sugar. By learning to read labels, you can determine how much sugar is in any food or beverage. To avoid a sneak attack, you should also learn the language of sugar, or the alternate terms food and drink manu-facturers use for it.

You can start by quitting the worst offenders—those items that have excessive amounts of the sweet stuff. Then stop consuming those empty-calorie sugary drinks and foods that you know are bad for you. While in the process of reducing your sugar intake, you should stop adding it to everything.

Keep the ball rolling toward better health by finding alternatives for the foods that you used to eat. It might be helpful to find a partner who can motivate and encourage you to quit sugar.

Having no sugar in your drinks and food takes some getting used to, so give your body time to adjust. Keep a journal where you record your battle with sugar. Then take the final steps to quit sugar for good, choosing your food wisely and reading labels to detect if sugar lurks in the ingredients list.

More Information

- Can Sugar Make Us Happy?[385]

- The Most Unhappy of Pleasures: This Is Your Brain on Sugar[386]

- Hold the Diet Soda? Sweetened Drinks Linked to Depression, Coffee Tied to Lower Risk[387]

385   http://greatist.com/happiness/can-sugar-make-us-happy

386   http://www.theatlantic.com/health/archive/2012/02/the-most-unhappy
-of-pleasures-this-is-your-brain-on-sugar/253341/

387   https://www.aan.com/PressRoom/Home/PressRelease/1128

52. Eat Less Trans Fat

Avoid eating large amounts of French fries, fried food, margarine, cake, frozen food, fast food, and snack foods. Yes, eating trans fat makes it more likely you'll die; but, more importantly, trans fat could make you less happy.

Eating more than 1.5 grams of trans fat per day can increase your risk of developing depression by 48%.

Forget about developing depression (although from personal experience, I can tell you it sucks more than almost anything else in the world); if trans fat can increase your risk of developing depression, it's likely making you less happy.

A 1o-year study of 12,059 participants[388] looked at two things: what people were eating, and whether they developed depression. After adjusting for biological differences—like exercise frequency, BMI, total energy intake, and age—those who ate the largest quantities of trans fat were 48% more likely to be diagnosed with depression within the next 10 years.

Notably, consuming large amounts of other types of fat, like saturated fat, had a much smaller effect.

As I mentioned earlier, nutrition science is a mess, which is why this tip is a maybe. The crap that comes out of that field is mind-boggling. A quick look at the food pyramid should make that obvious. We're supposed to get the majority of our calories from zero- nutrient insulin-spiking carbohydrates? No.

---

388   https://www.sciencedaily.com/releases/2012/03/120330081352.htm

Here's the problem—nutrition science often gets two things wrong:

1. It mixes up correlation with causation. For example, cholesterol is a symptom, not a cause of heart disease itself. For more on this topic, read Chris Kresser's article "The Diet-Heart Myth: Cholesterol and Saturated Fat Are Not the Enemy."[389]

2. It often has poor controls.

In the case of this study, income is not controlled for. Why does this matter so much?

As we discussed in the previous habit, the folks most likely to eat trans fat (e.g., cheap fast food) are those who are poor. Those who are poor are more likely to be unhappy and develop depression, for reasons that have nothing to do with their diet, like being unemployed or raising a child on their own.

But regardless of your socio-economic status, one small way you can increase your health *and* happiness is to cut back on the trans fat.

---

389 https://chriskresser.com/the-diet-heart-myth-cholesterol-and-saturated
-fat-are-not-the-enemy/

More Information

- Eating Trans Fats Linked to Depression[390]

- Inaccurate CDC Surveys May Make Our Nutrition Knowledge Bogus[391]

- Dietary Fat Intake and the Risk of Depression: The SUN Project[392]

390   http://www.webmd.com/food-recipes/news/20110126/eating-trans-fats
-linked-to-depression

391   http://www.bustle.com/articles/6740-inaccurate-cdc-surveys-may-make
-our-nutrition-knowledge-bogus

392   https://journals.plos.org/plosone/article?id=10.1371/journal.pone
.0016268

53. Skip the Diet

Sustaining weight loss is a lot like sustaining increased happiness: it requires a persistent change in the form of sustained changes to your day-to-day actions.

One-off events have a marginal long-term impact on happiness; the same is true with dieting.

I'm not trying to discourage you, just hoping that you'll apply effort where it's easier to make progress.

In most studies of dieters, those on a diet report higher well-being at the end. But in follow-ups months or years later, most report having gained back the lost weight and therefore having lost their increased self-esteem and happiness.

When considering the effort required for successful, sustained weight loss, dieting is no low-hanging fruit. In one study[393] combining data from five surveys across two countries and thousands of subjects, those identified as beautiful were 7% happier than those identified as ugly. Why so small a difference?

Instead, look for small ways to introduce simple healthy habits into your diet[394] instead of focusing on deprivation. You'd be surprised how small actions (like increasing your step count, adding more vegetables to your diet, or purging your home of "temptation foods") will not only make you happier, but will also help you cut down on your weight.

---

393   http://ftp.iza.org/dp5600.pdf
394   https://www.developgoodhabits.com/healthy-habits/

More Information

- Dieting Does Not Work, UCLA Researchers Report[395]
- Why Diets Don't Work ... And What Does[396]
- Predictors and Effects of Long-term Dieting on Mental Well-being and Weight Loss in Obese Women[397]
- The effect of weight-loss dieting on cognitive performance and psychological well-being in overweight women[398]
- Beauty Is the Promise of Happiness[399]

395 http://newsroom.ucla.edu/releases/Dieting-Does-Not-Work-UCLA -Researchers-7832

396 http://www.psychologytoday.com/blog/changepower/201010/why-diets -dont-workand-what-does

397 http://www.sciencedirect.com/science/article/pii/S0195666384710312

398 http://www.sciencedirect.com/science/article/pii/S0195666300903891

399 http://ftp.iza.org/dp5600.pdf

PART 6:

HOW TO BUILD THE HAPPINESS HABIT

8 Steps to Build a Happiness Habit

As you've seen, there are many, *many* ideas in this book. So it would be impossible to try them all. In fact, you only need to take action on a couple of strategies in order to increase your happiness. And that is why I recommend starting with the nine ideas I outlined in the "big levers of happiness" section.

Regardless of what ideas you focus on, building these happiness habits *will be hard*. Your brain doesn't make it easy for you. As much as you want to create a new habit and sustain it, your desire to keep at it begins to fade after a few days or weeks. At first, it's fun, then it's challenging, then it's work, and finally, it's forgotten.

Why does this happen?

It has nothing to do with your level of motivation. It has to do with brain chemistry. You haven't given your brain enough time to fully rewire itself to incorporate your habit as part of your daily routine. And that's what has to happen—you have to retrain your brain.

Furthermore, there is the problem called **ego depletion**, which is a person's "diminished capacity to regulate their thoughts, feelings, and actions," according to the book *Willpower*[400] by Roy F. Baumeister and John Tierney.

Our willpower is like a muscle. It weakens throughout the day because of constant use. You use your willpower when you make dozens of decisions each day. You use your willpower to

---

400 https://www.amazon.com/dp/B0052REQCY/ref=dp-kindle-redirect?_encoding=UTF8&btkr=1

concentrate at work. You use willpower to resist eating junk food. And you use willpower to resist lashing out at others when you're tired from a long day of work.

Because of ego depletion, your ability to form new habits is limited since there are only so many "new" things your willpower can handle at once. To keep things easy, we strongly recommend that you work on building *just* one habit for the next month, increasing the likelihood that you'll make this habit stick!

Most of us jump into a new habit full force. For example, if we decide we need to lose weight, we immediately change our diet, start exercising, write down everything we eat, and begin weighing ourselves.

But each one of these changes is comprised of a series of many smaller habits. By deciding to lose weight, you are asking your brain to accommodate 10 or more new habits rather than just one. Your brain can't handle that. It's like asking a toddler to pass advanced chemistry. No wonder we give up early.

But science has taught us there is a way to develop a new habit that minimizes the chance you'll throw in the towel. Here's what you need to do to turn a happiness habit into an automatic daily behavior—just like brushing your teeth, putting on clothes, and brewing your morning coffee.

1. Pick (and Stick to) a Happiness Habit

As you've seen, there are 53 ideas in this book. The problem? It's easy to feel *overwhelmed* by all the options. In fact, one of the main reasons people fail to take action on an idea is they don't enjoy the experience. And, in my opinion, people often quit because they didn't pick the *right* happiness habit.

So that's why the first step of the habit-building process is to review the 53 ideas I've profiled and pick one that best resonates with you.

Simply look at the table of contents and ask yourself: "Does this idea sound like something I'd *actually* like to do every day?"

There is no single idea in this book that's perfect for everyone. Your job is to find the idea that's *perfect for you*.

If your unhappiness is caused by constant fatigue, you should focus on getting a full night's rest (habit #7). Or if you feel constantly overwhelmed, you should consider using the 80/20 rule (habit #1) and/or subtracting unhappiness from your life (habit #2). Or if you're not living in the present moment, you'll get value from yoga (habit #20) and mindfulness meditation (habit #21).

The key point here is to pick an idea that adds value to *your* life. And more importantly, pick one that you're confident you'll *stick* to.

Some people say it takes 21 days to build a habit, while others claim it takes up to 66 days. The truth is that the length of time varies from person to person and from habit to habit. You'll find that some habits are easy to build while others require more effort.

My advice is to commit to one happiness habit for 30 days *at a minimum.* In other words, set aside time each day for the next month to focus on adding a little bit of happiness to your life.

2. Start *Really* Small

Most people want to create big change as quickly as possible.

They want to go from zero to four gym sessions every week, switch to a healthy diet overnight, and meditate for 20 minutes every day even though they've barely managed five minutes in the past. Biting off more than you can chew sets you up for failure.

Begin your new habit in small time bites. **Since this habit is new for you, focus on doing it for just a few minutes per day.** Do this for a week or so, and gradually add time over the successive weeks until it becomes a permanent behavior.

Always focus on establishing the actual *habit behavior* first and making it part of your day. Never increase the effort before it has become a natural part of what you do every day.

3. Use Activation Energy to Your Advantage

As Shawn Achor describes in *The Happiness Advantage*,[401] there is "activation energy" for each new habit. If you have too many hurdles and obstacles to begin a habit, you're less likely to take action on it.

Achor recommends **reducing the amount of activation energy required to start your new habit each day**. His rule of thumb is it should take no more than 20 seconds to begin a habit.

Here are a few ways to do this:

- If you'd like to practice gratitude, keep a journal at your bedside so you can start first thing in the morning.

---

401   https://www.amazon.com/Happiness-Advantage-Positive-Brain-Success-ebook/dp/B003F3PMYI/

- If you'd like to get more exercise, pack your gym bag the night before and have it ready to go when you leave for work.

- If you'd like to meet more people, schedule a meetup a week beforehand so there will be a social consequence if you cancel at the last minute.

Activation energy can work the other way as well—you can purposefully create barriers to bad habits that you'd like to break. If you need to jump through a bunch of hoops to continue a bad habit, you'll increase the likelihood of breaking it.

There are a few ways to do this:

- If you'd like to spend less time on your phone, leave it charging in another room before bedtime. (This will minimize the urge to look at it before you sleep *and* when you get up in the morning.)

- If you'd like to cut down on your Internet usage, use technology to block the websites where you waste the most time.

- If you'd like to cut down on alcohol, trans fats, sugar, and other types of unhealthy food options, make a rule to not keep it in your house.

Overall, there are countless ways to design your life for increasing good habits and decreasing bad habits. The trick here is to identify what causes you to fail with a specific habit and then structure your environment so you're making the right choices every day.

4. Identify a Trigger or Cue

Science has confirmed the best way to ensure you perform a new habit is by having a trigger that cues you to perform it. You mentally attach your new habit to this cue, and you have a built-in reminder system to get it done.

There are several different types of triggers you can use to do the job:

- **Time.** You can use a specific time of day as a reminder to perform your habit. For example, waking up in the morning or getting into bed at night could be your trigger to complete a specific habit. Or maybe you can do it just before or after your lunch hour.

  If you choose a random time, like 3:00 in the afternoon, you'll need to set an alarm on your phone or watch to remind you.

- **Location.** Research studies[402] by David Neal and Wendy Wood from Duke University have revealed that new habits are easier to perform in new locations. The theory is that since we already assign existing habits to specific locations, it's harder to consistently perform new habits in these locations because we're triggered to perform the old one.

  A new location gives you a blank slate that isn't associated with previous triggers for existing habits. I suggest you pick a specific location for your new happiness habit. This could be a quiet room in your house that's rarely used, or somewhere you go outside.

- **Previous Habits.** You can use an established habit as the trigger for your new habit. For example, you decided to

---

402   http://journals.sagepub.com/doi/abs/10.1111/j.1467-8721.2006.00435.x

complete a new habit immediately after you make your morning coffee or after you wash your face before bed.

This is part of the process of "habit stacking" I cover in my book by the same name (*Habit Stacking: 127 Small Changes to Improve Your Health, Wealth, and Happiness*).[403]

Just be sure you choose a habit trigger that you perform every day at about the same time. For a new habit to become automatic, you need to practice it every day in the beginning. A variable trigger that isn't daily will not help you remember to perform your habit.

5. Track Your Habit

It's not enough to anchor your new habit to another habit—you also need a mechanism to reinforce this behavior daily.

The simplest tool for building reinforcement is your mobile phone (since it's a device most people have on them throughout the day). We suggest you install one of three apps and use it to create reminders for practicing this habit.

- **Strides** (http://www.stridesapp.com): Strides has a clean, simple interface that allows you to track all your habits and goals.

- **Coach.me** (https://www.coach.me): This is another great tool. Not only can you use it to stick to your habits, but you can also connect with a coach to help you build a specific habit.

- **Chains** (https://chains.cc): Chains is built on Jerry Seinfeld's

---

403 https://www.amazon.com/Habit-Stacking-Changes-Improve-Happiness -ebook/dp/B06XP2B5QC/ref=sr_1_2?ie=UTF8&qid=1537208647&sr=8-2& keywords=habit+stacking

"never break the chain" concept, where you commit to a specific habit and never miss a day, creating a chain of positive behavior in your life.

Finally, if you're not interested in downloading a whole new app, you can also set a reminder to practice gratitude using one of these popular tools:

- Google Calendar (https://calendar.google.com)
- Evernote (https://evernote.com)
- Todoist (https://todoist.com)

Regardless of the tool you pick, we recommend keeping track of your habits by using some type of tool. You'll be surprised at how often the behavior of "checking in" makes the difference between whether you do or do not complete an action for the day.

6. Celebrate Your Small Wins

If you're like most people, you're much better at beating yourself up for a bad performance than you are at rewarding yourself for a good one.

When it comes to managing ourselves, for some reason, we seem to prefer the stick to the carrot. And that's a shame because research has shown that celebrating your progress is crucial for your motivation.

Each time you reward yourself for making progress, no matter how small, you activate the reward circuitry in your brain. That releases some key chemicals that make you experience feelings of achievement and pride. These emotions, in turn, empower you to take action and create bigger successes in the future.

So, reward yourself for each step in the right direction, no matter how small they happen to be. Whenever you complete a happiness habit for the day, reward yourself with something small.

Need some ideas? Consider these:

- Eat a piece of chocolate.
- Go outside and savor the fresh air.
- Call your best friend.
- Surf the net for a few minutes.
- Listen to your favorite song.
- Make a cup of tea and sip it slowly.
- Read a few pages of your book.
- Get a long hug from your spouse or partner.
- Close your eyes and rest for a few minutes.

There are countless ways to reward yourself for sticking to your new habit. If you'd like to learn more, check out my blog post,[404] "155 Ways to Reward Yourself for Completing a Goal or Task."

7. Surround Yourself with Supporters

The people around you have a surprisingly big impact on your behavior. One study[405] showed that if you have a friend who becomes obese, your risk of obesity increases by 57%--even if your friend lives hundreds of miles away!

Other research has shown that we tend to feel the same way and adopt the same goals as the people we spend the most time with. So, one way to dramatically increase your chances of

---

404   https://www.developgoodhabits.com/reward-yourself/
405   https://www.nytimes.com/2007/07/25/health/25iht-fat.4.6830240.html

success with your new happiness habit is to make sure you have the right people in your corner.

Be sure you have the support and encouragement of your spouse, partner, friends, and anyone who might know that you are committed to your new habit. Let them know that you're working to develop this habit, and ask them to encourage you and acknowledge your success with it.

8. Set Up Accountability

Many of us don't tell others when we begin a new habit because we don't want to be embarrassed if we fail. But public accountability can be a great motivator.

Accountability can be powered by integrity, fear of embarrassment, pride, or shame. Whatever the reason for using it, accountability works. It provides the element of tension to get the job done—to make something happen that might not have happened without it.

Announce your new habit on Facebook or other social media platform, or email all your friends to let them know. Then create a daily system of reporting your progress to these people.

Be sure you tell your accountability partner or group exactly how you want them to hold you accountable. Do you want to be called out if you haven't followed through? Or do you want only positive reinforcement when you get the job done? This is particularly important with your spouse and family members, as you don't want accountability to feel like shaming or nagging.

Final Thoughts on *Happier Human*

Our time together is almost complete.

You are now armed with over 50 ideas to increase your happiness. Some are small tweaks that require just a few minutes of your time, while others require a major commitment to change a significant part of your life.

I won't lie to you and say that all these ideas are easy, but they *do work* if you're willing to put in the effort.

As I discussed in the introduction, people often *say* they want to be happy, but their behavior and lifestyle are at odds with this desired outcome. So the biggest "secret" to becoming a happier human is to make sure your actions are in alignment with your happiness goals.

Simply put, if you want to be happy, you need to keep three simple rules in mind:

1. Focus on the things that truly matter.
2. Eliminate (or minimize) what makes you unhappy.
3. Create habits that help you achieve both these outcomes.

Happiness can be found when taking a personal inventory of your life and using these three rules to make better decisions. Start by giving some thought to the following questions:

- *Do you hate your job?* Then dedicate time to finding a better one, or look for a new career path.
- *Do you feel overwhelmed by too many tasks and obligations?* Then say NO to the things that don't matter to you.

- *Want to experience more personal fulfillment?* Look for volunteering options in your immediate area.

- *Hate the negative feelings you experience with certain friends and family?* Minimize the time you spend with these people, and join local meetups related to your personal interests.

- *Want to appreciate what you already have?* Practice gratitude and/or mindfulness to live more fully in the present moment.

If you're willing to spend a little time to better understand what makes *you* tick, it's not that hard to add a little bit of happiness into your day.

Now it's up to you!

I encourage you to *not* just close this book. Instead, pick just one idea from this book and take action. Use the eight-step habit-building process you just read in the previous section, and dedicate the next 30 days to turning this idea into a permanent habit. Once you're comfortable with that, add a second habit and then a third.

Sure, there will be times when you backslide. Occasionally, you will skip the habits you have scheduled for the day. But remind yourself that it's okay to fail and make mistakes. Just stick to the game plan!

Remember: perseverance is one of the true "secrets" to happiness.

I wish you the best of luck.

Steve "S.J." Scott

One Last Reminder ...

We've covered a wealth of information in this book, but that doesn't mean your journaling education ends here. In fact, we are offering a free digital product that's <u>exclusive</u> to readers of *Happier Human.*

If you'd like to get started right away, you can grab a PDF version of my co-authored bestselling physical journal:

The 90-Day Gratitude Journal: A Mindful Practice for a Lifetime of Happiness

Simple follow this link to grab your free PDF today:

https://www.developgoodhabits.com/90daygratitude

Thank You!

Before you go, we'd like to say thank you for purchasing our book.

You could have picked from dozens of books on habit development, but you took a chance and checked out this one.

So, big thanks for purchasing this book and reading all the way to the end.

Now we'd like to ask for a small favor. **Could you please take a minute or two and leave a review for this book on Amazon?**

This feedback will help us continue to write the kind of books that help you get results. And if you loved it, please let us know. ☺

More Books by Steve

How to Stop Procrastinating: A Simple Guide to Mastering Difficult Tasks and Breaking the Procrastination Habit

10-Minute Mindfulness: 71 Habits for Living in the Present Moment

Habit Stacking: 127 Small Actions to Improve Your Health, Wealth, and Happiness

Novice to Expert: 6 Steps to Learn Anything, Increase Your Knowledge, and Master New Skills

Declutter Your Mind: How to Stop Worrying, Relieve Anxiety, and Eliminate Negative Thinking

The Miracle Morning for Writers: How to Build a Writing Ritual That Increases Your Impact and Your Income

10-Minute Digital Declutter: The Simple Habit to Eliminate Technology Overload

10-Minute Declutter: The Stress-Free Habit for Simplifying Your Home

The Accountability Manifesto: How Accountability Helps You Stick to Goals

Confident You: An Introvert's Guide to Success in Life and Business

Exercise Every Day: 32 Tactics for Building the Exercise Habit (Even If You Hate Working Out)

The Daily Entrepreneur: 33 Success Habits for Small Business Owners, Freelancers and Aspiring 9-to-5 Escape Artists

Master Evernote: The Unofficial Guide to Organizing Your Life with Evernote (Plus 75 Ideas for Getting Started)

Bad Habits No More: 25 Steps to Break Any Bad Habit

Habit Stacking: 97 Small Life Changes That Take Five Minutes or Less

To-Do List Makeover: A Simple Guide to Getting the Important Things Done

23 Anti-Procrastination Habits: How to Stop Being Lazy and Overcome Your Procrastination

S.M.A.R.T. Goals Made Simple: 10 Steps to Master Your Personal and Career Goals

Made in United States
North Haven, CT
06 June 2023

37418922R00164